Text by Matthew Jones
Edited by Jeffery Pike
Design: Roger Williams
Series Editor: Tony Halliday

Berlitz POCKET GUIDE

Qatar

First Edition 2006

PHOTOGRAPHY CREDITS

Qatar Tourism Authority (QTA)/Rashed Ibrahim Al Muhannadi 6, 9, 10, 12, 15, 17, 20, 22, 28, 29, 30, 33, 36, 37, 39, 40, 43, 46, 52, 53, 57, 59, 61, 66, 70–1, 72, 73, 79, 80, 81, 82, 85, 87, 88, 89, 90, 93, 94, 95, 96, 99, 101, 105, 106, 107; Matthew Jones 2TR, 11, 18, 24, 27, 35, 38, 45, 49, 51, 55, 56, 60, 63, 64, 65, 69, 75, 76, 102, 107

Cover picture: mediacolor's/Alamy

CONTACTING THE EDITORS

Every effort has been made to provide accurate information in this publication, but changes are inevitable. The publisher cannot be responsible for any resulting loss, inconvenience or injury. We would appreciate it if readers called our attention to any errors or outdated information by contacting Berlitz Publishing, PO Box 7910, London SE1 1WE, England.

Fax: (44) 20 7403 0290;
email: berlitz@apaguide.co.uk
www.berlitzpublishing.com

Printed in Singapore by Insight Print Services (Pte) Ltd, 38 Joo Koon Road, Singapore 628990.
Tel: (65) 6865-1600. Fax: (65) 6861-6438

Berlitz Trademark Reg. US Patent Office and other countries. Marca Registrada

The Corniche in Doha (page 28) is the main sea-side promenade for taking a stroll

Doha (page 26) is the showcase for some impressive modern architecture

Al Zubara (page 74) is one of the country's many historic forts

TOP TEN ATTRACTIONS

Arabian thoroughbreds are put through their paces at the Racing & Equestrian Club (page 57)

Dhows at Doha Fishing Harbour (page 35)

Doha's *souqs* (page 38) are the place to find craftsmen at work

A desert safari can easily be arranged (page 83)

The Inland Sea (page 69) is a haunting stretch of water in the midst of dunes

The traditional houses and mosques of Al Wakra (page 64)

The Museum of Islamic Arts by renowned architect I.M. Pei (page 33)

CONTENTS

Fact Sheets

The Doha Buzz

In a recent ranking of the Arabian Gulf's top 10 business cities, the region's leading monthly business magazine, *Gulf Business*, listed Qatar's capital Doha as second only to Dubai, replacing Bahrain's capital, Manama, in the number-two spot. 'There is a buzz surrounding Doha,' said *Gulf Business*. 'Courted by multinationals, international banks and regional investors, Qatar and Doha City are suddenly flavour of the month. Or, if its assured gas-revenue streams are anything to go by, flavour of the decade.'

Qatar has huge reserves of natural gas. A major oil producer since 'black gold' was first produced in quantity in 1949, the country also contains the world's largest single gas field, and is currently its third-biggest gas producer. With global multi-billion-dollar gas deals filling the national coffers, Qatar has the fastest-growing economy in the region, and is the richest country in the world in terms of GNP per head of population.

Qatar's sporting calendar has a world-class golf tournament, a motorcycle Grand Prix and a thriving national football league featuring international big names. Its 2005 tennis champions, Roger Federer and Maria Sharapova, were the reigning champions at Wimbledon. Doha was also picked to host the 15th Asian Games in 2006, beating off competition from Kuala Lumpur and New Delhi.

Under the ruling Emir, Sheikh Hamad Bin Khalifa Al-Thani, the government is diversifying into sectors other than oil and gas – financial services, chemicals and tourism among them. Some $15bn is being invested in the construction of new tourism and cultural facilities. Qatar Tourism Authority (QTA), formed in 2002, is tasked with establishing Qatar as one of the world's leading quality destinations for leisure, business, education and sport.

Experiencing the buzz in Doha Bay

Leisure shouldn't be a hard sell. Qatar is blessed with a 563-km (350-mile) coastline – more than 200km (124 miles) of which comprises sandy beaches – and stunning natural attractions, such as the fabled Inland Sea (Khor Al Udaid), a 20-km (12-mile) wide tidal bay for which the government is seeking UNESCO World Heritage Site status. Qatar also offers year-round sunshine, though with temperatures peaking at 50°C (120°F) and high humidity in the northern-hemisphere summer, the best time to visit is between November and April, when the average hovers around a pleasant 25°C (74°F).

Changing Skyline

Doha itself, located halfway up the east coast of the Qatar Peninsula, is a fascinating destination that's at a turning point in its history. Shaking off its formerly sleepy, provincial air and unwelcome status as poor cousin to Dubai and Manama, the city is rapidly emerging as a vibrant international capital.

Coffee-pot sculpture

Nowhere is this more evident than in its changing skyline and architecture. Where the iconic, pyramid-shaped Sheraton Hotel dominated the sandy sweep of Doha Bay for much of the 1980s and 1990s, today its West Bay neighbourhood has numerous dazzling tall buildings that house national oil, gas and telecommunications companies, banks and financial institutions, the national Olympic committee headquarters and government ministries.

Among the recent additions to the Doha cityscape are new hotels. Following hard on the opening of the country's first independently owned luxury hotel in 2000, the InterContinental, a number of famous chains arrived in Doha in the early years of the 21st century. It's estimated that by 2010, the city will offer 10,000 rooms in 45 hotels, catering for the one million plus annual visitors expected by then – up from 400,000 tourists in 2004.

An increasing preference among Gulf-bound travellers for Arabian-themed accommodation is catered for in Qatar by the Sharq Village and Spa, constructed in the traditional Qatari style at the southern end of Doha's 7-km (4-mile) long Corniche, and the Al Fareej Resort, with its Arabian-style chalets, in the historic town of Al Khor, 40km (25 miles) north of the capital.

Other ambitious developments include the The Pearl Qatar land-reclamation project in West Bay Lagoon, which will have three luxury hotels and four marinas as well as freehold residential units; the $5.5bn New Doha International Airport, due for completion by 2015; and the ongoing expansion of the Qatar Airways fleet from 34 aircraft in 2005 to 59 by 2012.

Most notable among Qatar's architectural wonders are three landmark museum projects on Doha Corniche that are due for completion in 2006 and 2007: Isozaki's 120-metre (394-ft) high, futuristic National Library building, a magnificent, suspended, inverted pyramid; Pei's chunky, stone-clad Museum of Islamic Arts, which stands on its own artificial island; and Calatrava's ultra-light, wing-like Photography Museum.

Appealing Attractions

Iconic new buildings aside, Doha's Corniche – the focal point for the city's annual Cultural Festival every March – has long been one of the capital's most appealing attractions. In the late afternoon, as the sun dips behind the city, it's a favourite spot for walkers and joggers. Further inland, people-watching opportunities abound in the chic cafés and popular eateries around 'Ramada Junction' on Salwa Road, regarded by locals as the centre of Doha.

Nightlife for Qataris revolves around restaurants and coffee shops that serve *shisha* water pipes, or 'hubbly-bubblies', but Westerners tend to favour venues where alcohol is served. As the number of hotels has increased, so has the choice of

Shisha water pipes on the terrace of Al Bandar

bars. In a ground-breaking development in 2004, the sale of alcohol was licensed at a non-hotel venue – Amigo's Tex-Mex restaurant at the Khalifa Tennis and Squash Complex.

Outside Doha, notable attractions include the fishing port of Al Wakra and the Inland Sea to the south; to the north, the village of Umm Salal Mohammed, the fishing port of Al Khor and Al Zubara archaeological site and fortress; and the limestone outcrops and archaeological site at Zikreet to the west. Without a rail network or efficient organised public transport, the best way to see the country is by organised tour or hire car. Slightly smaller than the US state of Connecticut, Qatar is no longer than 200km (124 miles) north to south and 100km (62 miles) east to west, and can be covered easily in a series of day trips from Doha.

In terms of safety and security, crime in Qatar is virtually non-existent, and the country is largely untroubled by the tensions that affect others in the region. The only problem visitors are likely to encounter is 'Qatar time': paradoxically, while Qatar is amassing great wealth and undergoing dynamic improvements to its infrastructure, it's still very laid-back – the country virtually shuts down during the daily afternoon siesta.

The Barzan Tower at Umm Salal Mohammed

A BRIEF HISTORY

For a country that was established as recently as 1971, Qatar has a rich history that stretches at least as far back as 4000BC – to the New Stone Age or Neolithic period. The 5th–century BC Greek historian Herodotus knew enough about Qatar to claim in his chronicles that it was founded by the seafaring Kena'an tribes of the eastern Mediterranean, better known to us as the Biblical Canaanites.

Among the earliest evidence of human habitation on the peninsula are shards of prehistoric painted pottery identical to that of the Ubaid civilisation, which flourished along the Tigris and Euphrates rivers in southern Mesopotamia – present-day Iraq – in the period between 5600 and 3900BC. This 'Ubaid' pottery, first identified near Ur in the 1920s, was found at Ras Abaruk and Al Da'asa on Qatar's west coast by British archaeologist Beatrice de Cardi in the early 1970s. A subsequent French expedition in 1978 found more examples in Al Khor on the east coast. The discoveries indicate a clear link between the people of the southern Gulf and the pre-Sumerian Ubaid civilisation.

Further evidence of human activity in the Neolithic period comes from Danish, British and French studies of local flint tools. In an article for Qatar's *Gulf Times* newspaper in March 2005, reporting on a lecture by British archaeologist Dr Joan Oates, journalist Fran Gillespie provided a

Archaeologists believe that the discovery of 'Ubaid' pottery in coastal locations suggests that it arrived by sea – the earliest evidence of international trade anywhere in the world. There may have been a barter system, by which pottery was exchanged for locally produced dried fish.

fascinating insight into life in prehistoric Qatar: 'All the evidence so far discovered points to a highly developed, complex society at that time. The economy was based on fishing, the herding of sheep, goats and cattle, hunting and the gathering of wild food. Date palms are known to have been present in the Gulf then, as date stones have recently been found at an 'Ubaid'-related site on Dalma island just east of Qatar. The distribution pattern of the sites suggests that most of the year was spent inland where fresh water springs and grazing were available. The winters and early spring would have been spent on the coastal sites, fishing and gathering shellfish.'

Bronze Age

From the earliest days of international travel and commerce, then, Qatar has been strategically important. In the Bronze Age, from the third to the second millennium BC, the area is believed to have been one of the richest in the Gulf, as it benefited from the spread of culture and civilisation from Mesopotamia to the Indus Valley. The west coast, in particular, seems to have played a key role in the trans-shipment of materials via the Arabian Gulf, as evidenced by fragments of Barbar pottery found at Ras Abaruk, north of Zikreet. Barbar pottery is most commonly associated with Dilmun – present-day Bahrain – an island culture and important religious centre off Qatar's west coast that was itself a key port of call on the international trading route.

Qatar's trading links with powerful Mesopotamia continued when the Kassites emerged from the Zagros Mountains – in present-day western Iran – to take power in Babylon in the middle of the second millennium BC. Kassite-origin ceramics have been found at Al Khor. When the Assyrians gained power in Mesopotamia, late in the second millennium BC, the region would have continued to prosper.

Prehistoric carving at Jebel Jassiya

The Greek and Roman Era

By the time the Greeks arrived in the Middle East in the latter half of the 1st century BC, the Persians were running Babylon. When Babylon, and with it the Persian Empire, fell to Alexander the Great after the Battle of Gaugamela in 331BC, the way was open for a new era in trade between Europe and India via the Gulf. In 325BC, Alexander sent ships to explore its southern shores with the intention of adding Dilmun – known to the Greeks as Tylos – and the Arabian Peninsula to his empire. However, when he died in Babylon in 323BC, the area came under the influence of his successors, the Seleucids, but was never officially absorbed into the Greek world.

Qatar's fame among the ancients seems to have endured, nevertheless. In the 2nd century AD, the Greek geographer Ptolemy mentions 'Qatara' on his map of the Arab World. *Qatara* means 'drop' in Arabic, and there's speculation that

In the 1st century AD, the Roman writer Pliny the Elder referred to the area's nomads as 'Catharrei'.

the name may have originated in the valuable, drop-like pearls found off its coastline. Along with dried fish, pearls had become a key export by this period.

In the Roman era, archaeological evidence found on the Red Sea coast suggests that that waterway was favoured as the main route to India. This, combined with the development of overland caravan routes, may have led to a waning of Qatar's importance as a way station for international trade in the early years of the Christian era. However, archaeological evidence, again at Ras Abaruk, does indicate Greco-Roman influences in a stone dwelling, cairn and hearth. A low mound of fish bones from this era suggests the site may have been a temporary fishing station.

Sassanid Rule

The good times returned with the rule of the Sassanids – or Sassanians – the kings of Persia from the 3rd to 7th centuries. Under their rule, the coastal communities of the Gulf re-emerged as important hubs for East-West trade, with copper, spices, sandalwood and teak from the East being exchanged for shipments of gold, silver, dates and clothing. Qatar's own contributions to East-West trade were pearls and purple dye from seashells.

The Arrival of Islam

In the latter years of Sassanid rule, direct power over Qatar was wielded by the ruler of Bahrain, Al-Mundhir Ibn Sawa Al-Tamimi. In 628, Prophet Mohammad sent Al Ala Al-Hadrami as his envoy to Bahrain, inviting Mundhir to accept the new religion of Islam. Mundhir duly converted, and the inhabitants of Qatar soon followed. As Islam expanded out of Arabia in the mid-7th century, Qatari sailors played a key role in carrying Muslim soldiers across the Gulf to capture Persia. Qatar was famous for its woven robes at this time, which the Prophet Mohammed and his wife Aisha are believed to have worn.

Umayyad and Abbasid

The first of the Muslim Arab dynasties was the Umayyad Caliphate, which ruled from Damascus between 661 and 749, when the rival Abbasids seized power. The Abbasids would hold the caliphate until 1258, moving the capital from Damascus to Baghdad. Throughout this period, Qatar grew as a centre for trade and commerce, with Huwailah, on its northeast coast, emerging as a principal town. According to the Arabian historian Yaqut Al-Hamawi, who died in 1229, Qatar was famed for breeding camels and horses during the Umayyad

Pearls were exported as long ago as Greek times

period. During the Abbasid era, the pearling industry developed, with demand from as far away as China. Prosperity brought an increase in settlements in the north, such as at Murwab, where more than 100 small stone-built houses have been discovered. Murwab Fort bears the marks of the Abbasid architectural style.

The Portuguese and the Ottomans

In the early 16th century, the Qatar Peninsula – along with the rest of the western Arabian Gulf – came under Portuguese hegemony. Qatar fell to the Portuguese in 1515, and for the next 130 years its ports were used for the shipment of gold, silver, silks, musk, cloves, amber, pearls and horses to Europe. The history books record that in January 1625, Portuguese naval ships attacked Qatar's coastal villages. No doubt this was to protect their commercial interests, which may have been threatened by piracy, a problem encountered by a later imperial power.

Remains of the city wall at Al Zubara, once Qatar's main port

When the Portuguese were finally driven out of the Gulf by the Imam of Muscat in 1652, another major power, which had been waiting in the wings for some 300 years, stepped in to reinforce Islamic culture and exercise varying degrees of authority over Qatar until World War I – the Ottoman Turks. However, throughout the Ottoman period day-to-day rule lay in the hands of regional and local Arab rulers. In the 18th century, the Bani Khalid overlords of Kuwait controlled Qatar, with the port of Al Zubara their administrative headquarters.

British Influence

It was during the Ottoman era that Britain first made inroads into the region. Initially, its primary interest was economic, having established a British East India Company factory at Basra in 1635. But over the next 200 years, the political will to protect vital shipping lanes and overland routes to India hardened, and the British began to forge treaties with regional leaders to ensure protection from pirate attacks.

Qatar was excluded from the General Treaty of Peace with Arab rulers along the so-called 'pirate coast' in the 1820s, but was nevertheless expected to abide by its terms. In 1821, a British East India Company vessel flattened Al Bida (Doha) in retaliation for pirate attacks from the area. In 1835, Qatar signed a maritime truce that guaranteed the British freedom from attack during the pearling season at least, but by 1841, the situation was such that the British felt another shelling of Doha was needed to keep the populace in check.

Meanwhile, in 1766, the Al-Khalifa clan of the Utub tribe – originally from central Arabia, then Kuwait, where they had lived under the suzerainty of the Bani Khalid – settled in Al Zubara and became Qatar's rulers. When the Al-Khalifas moved to Bahrain in 1783, the British saw Qatar as a Bahrain dependency. However, when bitter fighting broke out between Bahrain and restive tribes in Qatar in 1867, leaving Doha virtually destroyed, the British came to recognise a new and powerful force in Qatari politics: the Al-Thani clan *(see panel on page 7)*.

The source of Qatar's booming economy

The Age of Al-Thani

By the 1860s, Sheikh Mohammad Bin Thani had emerged as one of the most important, and shrewdest, Arab leaders in the Gulf. On 12 September 1868, he signed a treaty with Col. Lewis Pelly, British Resident in the Gulf, in which Britain recognised the 'independence' of Qatar. However, for the next half-century the ruling Al-Thanis would play the British off against the Ottomans as and when it served their interests. In 1871, they invited the Ottomans to protect Qatar from external attack, and by 1872 the Ottoman occupation of Doha was complete.

Mohammad's son and successor, Sheikh Jassim Bin Mohammad Bin Thani, assumed the Ottoman title of Deputy Governor of Qatar in 1876, but the expansion of Ottoman administration in Al Zubara, Doha, Al Wakra and Khor Al Udaid, in addition to a custom house and strengthened garrison at Doha, led to open warfare between the Qataris and the

Ottomans in March 1893. At Wajbah, 15km (9.3 miles) west of Doha, Qatari fighters led by Sheikh Jassim defeated the Ottoman forces in a famous victory that signalled the beginning of the end of Ottoman authority on the peninsula. In 1915, they finally left, renouncing all rights to Qatar.

Regarded as the founder of modern Qatar, Sheikh Jassim died in July 1913, so it fell to his son, Sheikh Abdullah Bin Jassim Al-Thani, to negotiate a new treaty with Britain's Political Resident in the Gulf, Percy Cox. Signed in November 1916, the treaty guaranteed protection for Qatar 'from all aggression by sea'. On its part, Qatar undertook not to enter into relations with any other power without British consent and acknowledged the 'Trucial' system of administration that governed Britain's relations with other Gulf states.

'Black Gold'

Economically, the period between World Wars I and II was not a happy one for Qatar. The Wall Street Crash of 1929 led to a fall in demand for luxury pearls, but the death knell for Qatar's millennia-old industry came with Japan's development of the cultured pearl in the 1930s, which led to a 90 percent drop in value. Mercifully, another industry held some hope for poverty-stricken Qatar: in May 1935 it signed the 1st Oil Concession Agreement with the Anglo-Persian Oil Company.

The majority of Qataris are descended from three Bedouin tribes that moved to the peninsula in search of fresh water in the second half of the 19th century. But today Qataris constitute less than one-third of the country's total population. Economic growth in the 1970s and 1980s created an economy dependent on foreign workers, mostly from South Asia or other parts of Arabia, who now far outnumber nationals.

experience it. For all the activity associated with the government's mammoth $15bn investment in tourism infrastructure, it retains an unhurried charm. It's a beguiling place to unwind in, with plenty of stimulating attractions – modern, historic and cultural – that are never far away. Where better to begin looking for them than in Doha?

DOHA

Home to some 80 percent of the country's 840,290 population, Doha was once overshadowed by the trading port of Al Zubara, but has been Qatar's main city since the ruling Al-Thani family moved here from the northern town of Fuwairit in 1847.

Originally a fishing and pearling village called Al Bida, Doha was bombarded by the British in 1821 and 1841 for its alleged complicity in pirate attacks against British ships in the Gulf. In the 1867 war with Bahrain, Doha was virtually destroyed, and within five years was occupied by the Ottoman Turks. In 1916, when Sheikh Abdullah Bin Qassim Al-Thani concluded a treaty with Britain, Doha became the de facto capital of a British protectorate, the 'Trucial' state of Qatar, and remained the country's political centre after Qatar gained independence in 1971. Today, it's home to the executive, legislative and judicial branches of government (the Amiri Diwan, or ruler's palace, is midway along the Corniche).

With Qatar's main international airport less than 15 minutes' drive from the city centre and one of the country's three maritime ports off its Corniche, Doha is the gateway to Qatar for the vast majority of leisure and business travellers.

Orientation

East-facing – the sun rises in Doha Bay and sets behind the city – Doha is compact and easy to explore. Its attractions are never more than a short cab-ride away, and for visitors who prefer to drive themselves in hire cars, navigating is relatively straightforward. The city is laid out in a pattern of ring roads – named from A to E as you move from the centre to the suburbs – and bisecting main roads that eventually lead out of the city to the main towns in the north, south and west of the country.

The main streets in the city include the **Corniche**, which runs northward from the end of C Ring Road, near the airport, to the landmark, pyramid-shaped Sheraton Hotel in the West Bay district; **Grand Hamad Street**, which extends inland from the Corniche to A Ring Road and around which are located several of Doha's historic attractions and *souqs*; **Salwa Road**, which originates as Wadi Musheireb Street in the city centre and continues through Ramada Junction towards the fish and livestock markets beyond E Ring Road; and **Khalifa Street/Al Luqta Street**, which begins at 'Oryx

Watching a dhow pass by

Doha Corniche with the iconic Sheraton Hotel

Roundabout' behind the General Post Office and continues past the TV station and Education City towards Al Wajbah, Al Samariyah, Al Shahaniya and Zikreet.

Of the various roads leading north of the capital, Al Jamiaa Street from TV Roundabout offers the most direct route to Al Khor, while Al Shamal (North) Road from the Landmark Shopping Mall leads to the village of Umm Salal Mohammed and more distant Al Zubara.

The Corniche

For many visitors, the first sight of the Doha skyline comes as their car transportation rounds the corner onto the southern end of **Doha Corniche**, en route to one of the city's growing number of sea-facing hotels. Many of Doha's attractions are within walking distance of some part of this broad, pleasantly curving, tree-lined avenue on the edge of Doha Bay, but do consider that the Corniche itself is 7km

(4½ miles) long and is challenging to walk for any distance in the hotter months.

Instead of starting at one end and intending to walk its entire length with detours to various sights, it's recommended that you cab it to one of four key points: **Museum Roundabout**, also known as 'Perfume' Roundabout because of the perfume-bottle sculptures in the middle, which is near Qatar National Museum and the Ras Al Nasaa restaurant complex; the **Fishing Harbour**, which is just a few minutes' walk from either the new Museum of Islamic Arts, Al Koot Fort and Souq Waqif, or the Amiri Diwan and new Photography Museum; **Balhambar Restaurant**, which is near the new National Library site, the General Post Office and Khalifa Tennis & Squash Complex; or the area just before the **Sheraton Hotel**, where there's a jetty for a memorable trip around Doha Bay in a traditional dhow. From here, it's just a short walk between West Bay's tall buildings to City Center mall, one of the best in Doha, where you can get a refreshing drink in one of several international food outlets.

In the cooler months, between November and April, the Corniche is popular in the late afternoon with walkers, joggers and promenading families. At weekends (Thursday afternoons and Fridays), local and expatriate families alike gather on the grass area near the Sheraton for picnics and impromptu games of football, which Qataris are passionate about.

In March, the area around the Balhambar Restaurant, State Plaza, becomes the

Balhambar Restaurant

focal point for Doha's annual cultural festival, with dhow regattas taking place offshore and cultural performances in a temporary arena on the shoreline. Offshore, in Doha Bay, lies **Palm Tree Island**, a formerly barren sandbank that has been transformed into a family recreation and corporate hospitality centre, reached by a 10-minute dhow ride from the jetty near the Sheraton.

There's a small café/snack outlet near the dhow jetty, but other than this, with no shops fronting directly onto the Corniche, opportunities to buy refreshments are few and far between. Restaurants on the Corniche include the Balhambar, the Al Bandar group of outlets at the end of the Fishing Harbour jetty, and the Ras Al Nasaa complex on the southern end, towards the Marriott Hotel.

The Sheraton Hotel

Located in a local-style building that resembles a small fort, the Balhambar Restaurant (open daily noon–midnight) is named after a pearling area off Qatar's north coast. It specialises in traditional Qatari dishes – sweet and savoury – and has a delightful sea-facing terrace where locals gather in the evening to smoke *shisha* water pipes, or 'hubbly-bubbly'. The genuine appeal of Balhambar among Qataris and its delicious combination of local culture and cuisine ensure that a stop here is a must for all visitors, especially those who want to experience Qatar during the briefest of stays.

The *shisha* experience also awaits diners at the ship-shaped **Al Bandar** restaurants (open daily 12.30–11.45pm) further to the south. Al Bandar's Al Sharqi outlet specialises in Arabic appetizers, soups, grills and desserts, its Al Gharbi outlet in Indian Tandoori dishes, and its Fish Market outlet, naturally, in fish, including locally caught hammour, red snapper, kingfish and barracuda. A fourth Al Bandar outlet, Goroub, offers a bit of everything, and all are connected by a sea-facing terrace that brims with life on cool winter evenings.

Apart from the hotel restaurants on Ras Abu Abboud Street, the only other places to eat on the Corniche are at **Ras Al Nasaa**, a creative red-brick interpretation of a traditional Gulf wind-tower building that's just a five-minute walk from Qatar National Museum. Its **Al Jawhara Gallery** (open Sun–Wed 5–11.30pm, Thur–Sat 5pm–1am) offers authentic Arabic dishes as well as *shisha* on the terrace, which overlooks an attractive small marina and Doha Port. A second restaurant, Beach Palace (open daily noon–3pm, 6pm–midnight), serves Iranian cuisine.

One of the oldest landmarks on the Corniche, visible for its entire length, is the iconic 16-storey **Sheraton Hotel**, built in 1982, renovated at a cost of $20 million for its 20th anniversary in 2002, and still regarded by many as one of the best hotels in the Middle East. Royalty and heads of state, business tycoons and captains of industry, famous names in sport and show business, astronauts and admirals, economists and generals have all stayed here over the years. Distinguished names in the hotel guest book include US President George Bush, Egyptian President Hosni Mubarrak, the late Diana, Princess of Wales, Mohammed Ali and Bjorn Borg. On the top floor, the hotel's Al Shaheen fine dining restaurant (open daily 7pm–midnight) offers the best panoramic view of Doha Bay and Corniche.

In 2006 and 2007, this design icon is due to be joined on the Corniche by three landmark buildings that, at a stroke, are certain to propel Doha's once humble skyline to international attention. Rising to a height of 120m (395ft), with a built-up area of 45,000 sq m (approximately half a million square feet), **Qatar National Library** is set to tower over the General Post Office and National Theatre. A futuristic inverted pyramid supported on three mammoth pillars, it resembles an oil platform. The upper floors of the landmark structure will house the library itself, with space set aside for a Natural History Museum below. Isozaki's design also allows for art galleries, conference and lecture halls and a cafeteria and restaurant.

On the other side of Al Bidda Park, towards the Amiri Diwan, Calatrava's raised-wing **Qatar Photography Museum** is due for completion in 2007. Covering some 11,000 sq metres (118,400 sq ft) and rising to a height of 105 metres (345 ft), the structure will house photo and camera galleries, as well as galleries for temporary exhibitions,

International Architecture

Three of Doha's newest and most dramatic buildings are the work of architects from around the globe. The Qatar National Library was designed by the renowned Japanese architect Arata Isozaki, whose previous work in Qatar is the acclaimed Weill Cornell Medical College-Qatar, with its egg- and polyhedron-shaped lecture halls, at Education City *(see page 61)*. The Museum of Islamic Arts is the work of the Chinese-American I.M. Pei, who was responsible for the famous Pyramide du Louvre in Paris. And the Qatar Photography Museum is the creation of the famous Spanish architect Santiago Calatrava.

workshops, a library, the headquarters of Qatar Photographic Society, a shop, a cafeteria and a restaurant. Some 15,000 items, including the Bokelberg collection of historical photos and the Spira collection of vintage cameras, now owned by Qatar, are expected to be housed in the museum.

I.M. Pei's Museum of Islamic Arts

➤ Pei's **Museum of Islamic Arts**, towards Doha Port from the Photography Museum, near Water Pots Roundabout, is in many ways the jewel of the three. Though modest in height – it rises to just 60 metres (200ft) – it was designed to house priceless Islamic artefacts collected by the ruling Al-Thani family, in particular by the Emir's cousin, Sheikh Saud Al-Thani, the former President of Qatar's National Council for Culture, Arts & Heritage. As home to the world-class Qatar National Collection of Islamic Art, the museum showcases ceramics, metalwork, jewellery, woodwork and glass made in countries throughout the Islamic world, from medieval Spain to India and Central Asia. Pei, in his 80s, was reportedly coaxed out of retirement to design the five-storey, 45,000-sq m (484,390-sq ft) stepped structure, which stands on its own artificial island in Doha Bay. As well as gallery space, the museum has a library and study, restaurant, hanging gardens and water garden with fountain.

Ambient eateries and eye-catching landmarks aside, Doha Corniche has numerous other attractions. From Museum or Perfume Roundabout, it's just a short walk along Al Muthaf Street to **Qatar National Museum** (open Sun–Thur 9am–noon and 4–7pm, Fri 4–7pm; admission fee). Originally the home of the ruling Al-Thani family, the main building was built in 1901 by local architect Abdullah Al Mail in the pattern of a traditional Arabian palace. Its first resident was Sheikh Abdullah Bin Jassim Al-Thani, who ruled Qatar from 1913 to 1949. His son, Sheikh Ali Bin Abdullah Al-Thani, Qatar's ruler from 1949 to 1960, also lived here. Known as the Fariq Al Salata Palace, it opened as a museum in 1975, with themed exhibits on archaeology, natural history and oil and gas in various halls around a picturesque courtyard, a botanical garden and landscaped lagoon. But it went through a period of neglect in the early years of the 21st century – for a time it was closed to the public – until the government included an ambitious redevelopment of the site in its 2004 tourism master plan. The museum is

Fishing Boats

The common name given to wooden boats in the Gulf is dhow, from the Swahili word for boat, *dau*, but there are actually various kinds of dhow with variations in both appearance and name. Historically, the most common fishing boats in the northern Gulf were the *sanbuq*, *shu'i*, *jalbut* and *badan*. It's the *sanbuq* and, more popularly, the *shu'i* that are still in use today. In the 15th and 16th centuries, the Portuguese influenced boat-building in the Gulf, introducing iron-nailed framing in the hulls, but the construction techniques have changed little since then. Indeed, there's something distinctly Portuguese about the rise of the stern in the vessels tied up in Doha's fishing harbour.

A flotilla of boats in the Fishing Harbour

due to reopen in 2006 as a newly renovated showcase of Qatar's rich cultural history and heritage.

For a glimpse of an industry that's been a feature of the Qatar economy since the prehistoric Ubaid era – albeit a marginal one in the present age of oil and gas – head for the **Fishing Harbour**, which juts into Doha Bay near the junction of the Corniche and Grand Hamad Street (look for a distinctive pearl-oyster monument near the entrance). The flotilla of fishing boats moored side by side along the harbour wall, many patriotically flying the national flag, recalls a time when Qatar's naval fleet transported Al Ala Al-Hadrami's Muslim army across the Gulf to Persia.

The best time to see the daily catch being unloaded is early in the morning, but throughout the day there's some form of activity taking place in the harbour, from the mending of nets to engine repairs or the construction of the domed wire gargoor fishing traps that are placed on the seabed overnight. If the sight of fishing dhows whets your appetite for a jaunt around the bay, the place to catch a ride on a passenger boat isn't here, but at the dhow jetties near the Balhambar Restaurant and the Sheraton. Generally, they sail from 4pm daily.

A five-minute walk from the Fishing Harbour, in the direction of the Sheraton, is the **Amiri Diwan**, or ruler's palace. Set back slightly from the road, this imposing building – the Emir's 'working' palace – isn't open to the public.

For greenery on the Corniche, the 'Sheraton Playground', in a public area near the eponymous hotel, offers decent swathes of grass for a rest or run-around, and plenty of shade under its palm trees. For more things to do, however, head for **Al Bidda Park** (open daily early morning to late night), which is just over the busy Corniche road, between the National Library and Photography Museum sites. Linking the old city centre to the bright new West Bay district, Al Bidda Park is a pleasant family destination, with something for all ages, from a small train and boating pool for young children, to a 'halfpipe' for teenage skateboarders and rollerbladers, to an art gallery for mum and dad that has regular exhibitions of paintings, photographs, ceramics and sculptures by local, regional

Handfuls of fish

and international artists. The park also has several mock heritage buildings, a small market and café.

The Old City Centre

Just inland from the Corniche, in an area roughly bordered by Al Bidda Street, Al Diwan Street, the A Ring Road and Jabr Bin Mohammad Street, lies the heart of Doha, the old neighbourhoods from which the city has expanded over the last half-century.

The Clock Tower

Between the decorative **Clock Tower**, which stands alongside the Amiri Diwan, and Dhow Roundabout on Jasim Bin Mohammed Street, stands the Moorish-style **Al Koot Fort**, otherwise known as Doha Fort (open Sun–Thur 7am–noon and 4–7pm, Fri 4–6.30pm). One of the few remaining military forts in Doha, Al Koot was constructed on a small hill overlooking the Al Bidda area in 1917, during the reign of Sheikh Abdullah Bin Jassim Al-Thani. Like Sheikh Abdullah's former home – now Qatar National Museum – his former castle has undergone an extensive renovation in recent years and is now **Qatar's Museum of Traditional Costumes and Textiles**. The Scottish architect Kathryn Findlay, of the London-based Ushida-Findlay architectural practice, was given the task of renovating the historic building. Her design conserved the fabric of the fort, well known for its ornately carved gypsum plaster decorations, but inserted a new core. Most of the museum's 6,500 sq m (70,000 sq ft) of floor space is underground to the front of the fort. Jacqueline

Simcox, a London-based expert in Asian fine arts and an internationally respected authority on textiles, was the project's curatorial consultant.

Across the public car park from Al Koot Fort is Doha's most atmospheric old market, **Souq Waqif** (open Sat–Thur 9am–1pm, 4–8pm, Fri 4–8pm), the site of which was the original weekend 'standing *souq*', where Bedouin tribespeople once traded their meat, wool, weaving and milk for goods not available to them in the harsh desert interior. Though popular with tourists, Souq Waqif is very much an active market, its maze of covered alleyways busy with Qataris shopping for spices, perfume, incense and traditional clothes, including *bishoot* (ceremonial, gold-edged cloaks for men), *abayat* (women's cloaks) and *bukhnoq*, exquisitely embroidered head-coverings, decorated with gold and silver thread, that are traditionally worn by Qatari girls. *Shisha*

Souk Waqif, where Bedouin tribesmen once traded

Sewing in the *souq*

pots, pipes and accessories are available in the *souq*, as are camel blankets, each of which has a hole for the hump. More practically, Souq Waqif is also a source of inexpensive kitchenware, towels and linen, clothing and shoes, tools and DIY items, pushchairs and bikes. Remember, haggling for the best price isn't just accepted, it's expected.

An interesting feature of life outside the *souq* are the numerous wooden booths that are occupied either by cobblers busily repairing shoes or by typists creating official documents in Arabic for those who can't read or write the language. Also of interest are the raised traffic islands from which policemen, dressed in colonial-style uniforms with Arabic headdress, direct both drivers and pedestrians. They don't mind being photographed, but ask beforehand.

Other more modern *souqs* are clustered around nearby Grand Hamad Street. **Souq Al Ahmad**, adjacent to Souq Waqif, is a modern, two-storey, air-conditioned building with stores selling perfume, clothing, linen, electrical items and household goods. In particular, the *souq* contains several ladies' tailors specialising in bridal and evening wear with intricate beadwork.

Also near by, along Al Ahmed Street, there are a number of other contemporary buildings containing *souqs*, including Souq Faleh, Souq Nasser Bin Saif, Souq Al Asiery, which is particularly good for cheap fabrics, Doha Souq, Souq Al

Basket-weaver at work

Dira, known for upmarket textiles, beaded fabrics and heavy lace, and Souq Al Jabor, which actually feels more like a small mall than an Arabian *souq*.

The **Gold Souq**, such as it exists, is a cluster of small jewellery shops on a small road behind Al Ahmed Street and extending into nearby alleyways. Even if you're not intending to purchase, the Gold Souq is still an interesting place to visit, particularly in the evening, when the area is at its liveliest. Most of the items in the window displays are made of 22-carat gold, which is especially popular in the Gulf region. With the exception of elaborate Qatari bridal jewellery and some other locally made items, in

Bedouins were renowned for their weaving skills and traditionally produced a variety of woven items, from fine capes to saddlebags, blankets and large camel- or goat-hair tents.

which decorative glass is sometimes used instead of precious stones, much of what's on offer is imported, though the prices are generally lower than in the West. One or two vendors may have Bedouin jewellery for sale, but if you're interested you should ask: it's not always on display.

Should you feel peckish when you're shopping in old Doha's *souq* area, **Thai Noodles** (open daily 8am–11pm), opposite Souq Al Asiery, is one of the most popular value-for-money restaurants in Doha. Even if you're not in the immediate vicinity, consider taking the short detour from the Corniche: the restaurant is in the street behind the Ministry of Finance building.

Not far from the grouping of *souqs* on Al Ahmed Street, **Souq Al Najada** stands on the corner of Grand Hamad and Al Bin Abdullah streets, a short walk up the latter from Dhow Roundabout. Not as old or as architecturally appealing as Souq Waqif, it does, nevertheless, boast a site of special interest: Qatar's last remaining original **Wind-Tower House** *(see below)*. Built in 1935 as a private residence, it stands alone in a small plaza in the *souq*. Formerly the

Ancient Air Conditioning

The building which now houses the Gulf Architectural Heritage Centre has a distinctive feature that was once common in Qatar – a square, open-sided tower rising from one corner. Known locally as a *badghir*, this is actually an early form of air conditioning, introduced to the coastal communities of the southern Gulf by traders from Iran. The sides of the tower were designed to catch what breeze there was from any of four directions and channel it down to the ground-floor rooms. The air could be further cooled by stretching damp fabric across the bottom of the tower – an ingenious way of keeping the temperature down in the days before electricity.

Ethnographic Museum, the building is now the Gulf Architectural Heritage Centre. Officially, the house is no longer open to the public, but during office hours its heavy wooden door is open, and the staff inside are quite happy for visitors to wander around its small courtyard.

Just north of Al Bidda Street, on a side road parallel to Majlis Al Taawon Street, is the Rydges Plaza Hotel, which has a first-rate rustic-style Italian restaurant, Il Rustico (open daily 11am–3pm and 6pm–midnight), and one of Doha's most popular late-night venues, Aussie Legends (open Sat–Thur 4pm–3am, Fri noon–3am). Themed around the legends of Australian sport, the bar serves one of the best burgers in town, has a dance floor and adjoining pool terrace, and shows all the major international sporting events (rugby, football, cricket and Formula 1) on a big screen.

West Bay

While there's still plenty of life in the streets of the old city centre, much of Doha's government, business and leisure activities have gravitated to a new high-rise district which has risen to prominence since 2000: West Bay.

Beginning at Al Bidda Park, West Bay – much of which is actually to the north of the city – is Doha's new commercial hub, home to the towering offices of the nation's banks, oil-and-gas and telecommunications companies. The ministries of Interior, Justice and Economy and Commerce are here, as are the country's Law Courts and a number of foreign embassies. On its southwest fringe is the **Khalifa Tennis & Squash Complex**, the venue for the ATP and WTA tennis tournaments, while at the tip of the West Bay Peninsula, behind the Sheraton, are Qatar International Exhibition Centre, venue for the World Trade Organisation's 4th Ministerial Conference in 2001, and the new West Bay Complex, which has one of Doha's tallest office buildings, the 158-m (518-ft)

Tennis championship match at the Khalifa complex

headquarters of local telecom provider Qtel, and a luxury Four Seasons Hotel. Also in West Bay is one of Qatar's most fashionable malls, **City Center Doha**, which has international brand-name stores, a large Starbucks and one of the few ice rinks in the Middle East.

The Khalifa Tennis & Squash Complex, with its impressive Centre Court, is in the grounds of the Al Dana Club, on the other side of the General Post Office from the Corniche. In January, it hosts the annual men's ATP Qatar Open tennis tournament, a world-class event that has attracted the likes of Pete Sampras, Boris Becker and Roger Federer in their prime. The separate annual women's WTA Qatar Open takes place here in late February and counts Grand Slam queens Martina Hingis, Monica Seles and Maria Sharapova on its roster of champions. Every April, the famous veterans of men's tennis come here to compete in the ATP's international Champions Tour event.

But the complex is a lively destination even when it's not hosting top tennis. The casual, American-style family restaurants Fuddruckers (open Sat–Wed 11am–midnight, Thur 11am–1am, Fri noon–midnight) and Bennigan's (open Sat–Wed 11.30am–11.30pm, Thur 11.30am–12.30am, Fri noon–12.30am) are here, as is the more formal Indian tandoori Bukhara (open Sun–Wed 11.30am–2.30pm and 6–11.30pm, Thur–Fri 11.30am–3pm and 6pm–midnight, Sat 11.30am–3pm and 6–11.30pm). One of Doha's most popular nightspots is also here – Amigo's Tex-Mex restaurant (open daily noon– 3am), which is unique in that it's in neither a private club nor a hotel venue and yet is licensed to serve alcohol. Amigo's also offers live entertainment, with a resident British band, and shows live sports on several TVs dotted around the bar and lounge areas.

The **Al Dana Club** itself is one of Doha's venerable members-only institutions; it was founded in 1975, and is just around the corner from Amigo's. Located in a white-painted, traditional-style building, its recreational facilities aren't open to non-members, but its restaurants are. The club's fine-dining Lewan Restaurant (open daily noon–3pm and 7pm–midnight) serves alcohol with its Lebanese hot and cold *mezze* and Middle Eastern, Oriental and European main courses.

West Bay is worth venturing into for its architecture alone. The architect behind the Al Dana Club in the 1970s was the Qatari Ibrahim Jaidah, and his present company, the Arab Engineering Bureau (AEB), is responsible for many of Doha's modern landmarks. AEB's design approach, which evolved in the 1990s, is to reflect the current development of Qatar while also preserving and expressing traditional Qatari architecture, where appropriate. Near the Al Dana Club is the 21-storey **Barzan Tower**, designed by AEB for local client Abdullah Bin Khalifa Al Attiyah and completed in

2000. Though not open to the public, it's beautiful to study from the surrounding streets. Inspired in part by the architecture of an old defensive tower of the same name in the town of Umm Salal Mohammed *(see page 64)*, the lower part of the building has a traditional look, while the upper floors rising out of it consist of ultra-modern blue glass. In the words of Ibrahim Jaidah, 'The lower floors come from our culture, while the blue glass reflects our future.' Qatar's Ministry of Housing and civil service are based in the building.

The trend for combining local Arabic and modern influences is popular among other designers. The distinctive, 23-storey **Al Waqf Tower**, near City Center mall, built in 2002 to house the Ministry of Education, has an Islamic-influenced white dome cut into its imposing glass-and-concrete façade. On the shoreline, the **West Bay Complex**, designed by the American firm Smallwood, Reynolds, Stewart, Stewart & Associates and completed in 2005, was influenced by Qatari and Moorish architecture, in particular the Alhambra palace-citadel in Granada, Spain, which combines elements of fortress, residential area and palace into one complex. As well as a 28-floor office tower, occupied by Q-Tel and boasting the fastest elevators in Doha (they move at five metres per

Al Waqf Tower

The InterContinental Hotel, a popular Friday meeting place

second), the development has two 22-level apartment blocks, 20 three-storey townhouses and a 20-storey, five-star Four Seasons hotel with private beach and 110-berth marina. The Four Seasons offers elegant indoor and open-air terrace dining, including an all-day French brasserie and Italian fine cuisine, as well as a pool bar and grill, and library bar and cigar lounge. The hotel also boasts a luxury spa.

Not only is West Bay growing upwards, it's also growing outwards, in the less built-up area along Lusail Street/Al Istiqlal Street, which heads north out of Doha towards the MotoGP circuit. The InterContinental and Ritz-Carlton hotels are here, as is the Aladdin's Kingdom entertainment park and Doha Golf Club.

At the **InterContinental Hotel**, which opened in 2000, the Amwaj buffet-style restaurant (open Sat–Thur 12.30–3.30pm and 7–11.30pm, Fri 11.30am–4pm and 7–11.30pm) is a popular venue for Friday brunches among both Qataris and resident expats – Friday being the equivalent here to Sunday in the West. The hotel also has a lively Tex-Mex, Paloma (open daily 6pm–midnight for dinner, midnight–2am for dancing), an oriental-style seafood restaurant, Sultan Ibrahim (open Sun–Fri 1–3.30pm and 7pm–midnight), and one of Doha's most stylish Italian restaurants, Za Moda (open Sat–Thur 12.30–3.30pm and 7pm–midnight, Fri 7pm–midnight).

For the young and young at heart, **Aladdin's Kingdom** (open daily 4–11pm; admission fee), next to the InterContinental, is Doha's premier entertainment park, with 18 rides and activities for all age groups, including a small – but very noisy – roller-coaster.

North along the coast, near the causeway entrance to the Pearl Island land-reclamation project, the 115-m (377-ft) Ritz-Carlton Hotel, completed in 2001, also has a number of superb restaurants. Offering a fine view of the Arabian Gulf from the top floor of the 23-storey tower, La Mer (open Sun– Tues 6.30–11pm, Wed–Thur 6.30–11.30pm, Fri noon–2.30pm) is the hotel's opulent signature restaurant, serving French cuisine. Below the lobby level, Porcini (open Sat–Tues 6.30–11pm, Wed–Thur 6.30–11.30pm) is the hotel's formal Italian restaurant. For more casual dining with a view of the Gulf, try the ground-level Lagoon restaurant (open daily noon–3.30pm and 6.30–11.30pm), another popular venue for long Friday brunches among locals and expats. Parents take note, the Lagoon has a special menu for children. Alternatively, if you just want to take tea at the Ritz, you might want to coincide your visit with a Tea With A Twist

Next to Aladdin's Kingdom is the Cultural Village, a purpose-built centre that's designed to give citizens and foreign visitors a taste of how previous generations lived on the peninsula and to showcase local arts and crafts.

fashion show that takes place in the lobby lounge from 2.30–5pm on the second Thursday of every month.

Located just north of West Bay Lagoon, 8km (5 miles) from City Center mall, **Doha Golf Club** is the venue for the annual $1.5 million PGA European Tour Qatar Masters in March. The clubhouse will appeal to golfers and non-golfers alike. Designed in the Arabian style of an opulent Qatari home, with marble interiors, handmade gypsum detailing and solid teak doors imported from Thailand and locally engraved, the clubhouse has two public restaurants: the ground-floor **Spikes Lounge** (open Sat–Thur 10am–midnight, Fri 8am–midnight), a stylish fusion between bar and club, and the more traditional Oasis Lounge (open Sat–Thur 6.30am–midnight, Fri 6am–midnight; dress code), on the first floor, which has an attractive open-air terrace overlooking the ninth and 18th greens.

If you're relying on taxis for transportation, getting to the InterContinental, Ritz-Carlton or golf club from the more cen-

Lush Fairways in the Desert

The Qatar Masters is a world-class golf tournament which has attracted the top names in the game, including Ernie Els, the champion in 2005. Designed by Peter Harradine, one of the world's leading golf-course architects, the Doha Golf Club's challenging 18-hole Championship Course measures 6,686m (7,312yds), its 150 hectares (369 acres) of lush fairways and greens created from barren desert in the 1990s by the planting of grass, 1,300 palm trees, 10,000 other trees, 5,000 shrubs and 65 cacti specially imported from Arizona. For less experienced or novice golfers, the club's nine-hole floodlit Academy Course is a less demanding 2,600m (2,844yds). Non-members and visitors can play either course, and individual coaching for men, women and juniors is available at the club's Doha Golf Academy *(see page 85)*.

Doha Golf Club, venue of the PGA European Tour Qatar Masters

tral parts of West Bay won't be a problem – if you can't hail a cab on the street, you're sure to find one at the taxi rank outside City Center mall. But be aware that finding a cab for the journey back isn't so easy – few cabs wait at any of the three locations, and the hotels' 'limousine' service costs a premium. The most cost-effective option is to book a Karwa taxi well ahead of time, but be prepared to wait *(see page 114)*.

Back among the high-rises of West Bay proper, **City Center Doha** (open Sat–Thur 10am–10pm, Fri 3–10pm) is a five-storey mall that offers a welcome escape from the sun at any time of year. Entertainment-wise, as well as having an ice rink in its central atrium – part of a year-round **Winter Wonderland** attraction – the mall has a small indoor **Water Park** for kids, an eight-lane **10-pin bowling centre** for all age groups, an **Internet City** for young children and teenagers and a multi-screen **cinema**. In addition to a large Debenhams and the variety of international brand name stores you would expect to find in any modern city, the mall has a large Carrefour supermarket (good for competitively priced travellers' essentials, such as water and tissues, as well as Western newspapers), various cafés and coffee shops, and a food court with Nando's, Applebee's and Pizza Express restaurants. Among the various fast-food outlets is Tazaj, a chain that's popular throughout the Gulf for its good, value-for-money chicken meals.

Ramada Junction

Moving inland, one of Doha's most unlikely tourist attractions is the interchange of C Ring Road and Salwa Road, popularly known as '**Ramada Junction**', due to the fact that the hotel is located near by. There's actually nothing to see here in terms of historic sites, or do here in terms of vacation activities, but therein lies its appeal: Ramada Junction is where Qataris and resident expats come to unwind, and its coffee shops and restaurants present visitors with wonderful opportunities to fall in step with the pace of life here (mostly unhurried), to people-watch and perhaps even talk with locals, who regard this area as the centre of Doha.

By far the most stylish contemporary eatery at Ramada Junction is **Café Le Nôtre Paris** (open Sat–Thur 8am–11.30pm, Fri 8–11am, 12.30–11.30pm), next to the Al Emadi Center on Salwa Road. Here, members of Doha's in-crowd – men and women in national dress and style-conscious Arab expats from the Levant – sit on the terrace to see and be seen, sipping smoothies, granitas

Culinary delights aside, Ramada Junction also has a good bookshop, the Jarir Bookstore, which is open 8am–1pm and 4–10pm Sat–Thur, 4–10pm Fri. It sells books and magazines in English as well as Arabic and has a good selection of stationery items.

Café Le Nôtre Paris, a stylish eatery

and shakes while they chat or text friends to the beat of modern mood music piped through 'rocks' in the cafe's rockeries. The cars parked outside are invariably of the Hummer-Ferrari-BMW variety.

Behind Café Le Nôtre, Ma Maison Salon de Thé (open daily 8am–midnight) is a much more traditional French patisserie and chocolaterie with a small but elegant Parisian-style tea lounge. The funky Crepaway (open Sat–Wed 6.30am–12.30am, Thur–Fri 6.30am–1.30am), on the other side of the Al Emadi Center, is popular with Lebanese familiar with the chain from Beirut. One of Doha's ubiquitous Starbucks outlets is a stone's throw from all three venues.

Family restaurants are well represented on virtually all corners of Ramada Junction. On the same side as Café Le Nôtre, there's Ponderosa steak house (open Sat–Thur 11.30am–midnight, Fri noon–midnight). Across Salwa Road, a short walk along C Ring Road, you'll find a large

Chilis (open Sat–Wed 11am–midnight, Thur–Fri 11am–1am). Options for more formal dining in the area include The Beijing (open daily 11.30am–3.30pm and 5.30–11.30pm) on Salwa Road, probably the best Chinese restaurant in town, and, at the Ramada Hotel itself, the French Maxim (open daily 7–10.30pm), The Italian Job (open daily 7–10.30pm), the Japanese Sakura teppanyaki and sushi bar (open daily 7–10.30pm) and the Indian Chingari Tandoori restaurant (open daily 7–10.30pm). Of all the venues mentioned, only the last four, at the Ramada Hotel, serve alcohol.

A short drive southwest from Ramada Junction, heading out of the city along Salwa Road, Al Layali Restaurant (open daily noon–midnight) offers traditional Lebanese dishes in an atmosphere that's wonderfully evocative of the old Levant and Arab North Africa. Located in Souq Najd, Al Layali – which means 'Nights' in Arabic – uses only

Large shopping malls are part of modern Doha

Shopping in The Mall

fresh herbs from Lebanon to accentuate its delicious array of lamb, chicken and fresh fish entrées. Not only does the restaurant offer the best Lebanese food in town – the Emir himself has been known to drop in – it's also known for the quality of its *shisha.*

Cafés dotted along this same stretch of Salwa Road, between Ramada Junction and the Al Asiri Interchange, include Lina's (open Sat–Thur 10am–midnight, Fri 5pm–midnight) and Café Hediard (open Sat–Thur 9am–12.30am, Fri 1pm–12.30am), but the pick of the bunch has to be Café Batteel (open daily 8am–midnight), a friendly eatery with a typically regional ambience that offers fine dining as well as coffee, pastries and Arabic sweets.

Around D Ring Road

Continuing inland, D Ring Road – which begins near the airport and changes its name to Al Amir Street at Al Asiri Interchange and to Al Shamal (North) Road in the Al Luqta neighbourhood – marks the beginning of Doha's outer fringes.

Large malls at either end of the road should satisfy shoppers. Nearest the airport, **The Mall** (open daily 9am–noon and 4–9pm) was the first suburban mall in Doha when it was built in 1997. It has 45 retail outlets and a cinema. However, **Landmark Shopping Mall** (open Sat–Thur 9am–10pm, Fri 3–10pm) at the northern end of the road is much larger and brighter, and offers more international stores, including

Marks & Spencer and BHS – though the style gurus of Ramada Junction would favour Massimo Dutti and Esprit. Landmark also has a multi-screen cinema, Circusland entertainment centre for young visitors and a large food court: look out for the Yum Yum Tree outlet, in particular, which specialises in excellent, value-for-money pastas and stir-fries.

Also on D Ring Road, not far from the US embassy compound, is the **Weaponry Museum** (tel: 486 7473; open Sun–Thur 7.30am–noon). Located in a converted villa on Al Maha Street, behind Souq Al Ali at the Al Gharrafa Interchange (look for the small cannons outside), the museum houses rare examples of gold and silver swords, curved Arabian *khanjar* daggers, exquisitely inlaid pistols, jewel-encrusted rifles, bows and arrows and armour, some of which dates back to the Portuguese era in the 16th century. Weaponry-related paintings and photographs are also on display.

The Weaponry Museum, which is based on the private collection of Sheikh Hassan Bin Mohammed Bin Ali Al-Thani, has been known to refuse entry to independent travellers who turn up on spec, so it's recommended that you either arrange your visit with a tour group or phone ahead to make an appointment.

Two roundabouts south-west of D Ring Road, along Salwa Road and left on Wholesale Market Street, Doha's separate Thursday and Friday, Omani, fish and livestock markets are well worth visiting for the experience alone. Clothes, fabrics, shoes, household goods and carpets are available in the permanent shops at the **Thursday and Friday Market** (open 7am–noon and 4–10pm). Generally, the quality of the products is low, but then so are the prices. Between October and March, the falcon-hunting season, the *souq*'s three falconry shops display the birds as well as the leather gloves, hoods

Stalls at the Omani Market sell a variety of regional products

and accessories, but the most valuable hunting falcons are usually traded in private. Only one of the shops has a sign in English, Al Jazeera Falcons. Across the street, behind the large fruit and vegetable market, the covered stalls of the **Omani Market** (open daily 6am–10pm) have incense, dates, nuts and honey from the region; palm-frond baskets, mats and boxes; locally made pottery; and walking sticks and camel crops.

If you can stand the whiff, the **Fish Market** (open daily 6am–2pm) on Haloul Street is a hive of activity, particularly early in the morning when local restaurateurs make their bulk purchases – by the box rather than the kilo – and its corridors become jammed with porters pushing wheelbarrows full of fish towards the buyers' waiting trucks. Numerous species of fish and shellfish, of all sizes, shapes and colours, freshly caught in the Gulf, are displayed on ice in the market's noisy halls – if you're not planning to go scuba diving or deep-sea fishing during your visit to Qatar, this will be your one chance to inspect them. You might even see a shark.

The senses are also assaulted at the **Livestock Market** (open daily 6am–6pm; some traders open earlier and finish later), a timeless animal bazaar that's a little further along Wholesale Market Street. Here, highly prized camels, cattle, sheep and goats are sold from pens as they have been for generations, but there are also rabbits, chickens, ducks and geese to see. The caged birds on sale in the market's **Bird Souq** (open daily 7am–noon, 3–6.30pm) include spotted guinea fowl, ring-necked parakeets and large African grey parrots. Generally, there's nothing that will upset even the most sensitive animal-lover at the animal-and-bird *souq* – the pens are large enough, straw and water are provided and a nearby municipal office ensures they're healthy and well cared for – but you won't be the first

The Livestock Market

Hospitalised falcon

visitor to wonder why on earth the chicks in the bird *souq* have been dyed pink, yellow and green.

Sticking with the animal theme, **Qatar Falcon Center**, a hospital for sick and injured falcons, is one roundabout further along Salwa Road. Although not officially open to the public, when they aren't busy its staff have been known to give curious passers-by a glimpse of the operating room and three 'wards' where falcons are treated for a variety of ailments, from dietary problems to foot injuries and broken bones.

For larger and more exotic animals, head for **Doha Zoo** (open daily 8am–noon and 3.30–8.30pm in summer, 8am–noon and 2.30–7.30pm in winter; admission fee) on Al Furousiya Street, which is off Fort Roundabout on Salwa Road. Set in 17 hectares (40 acres) of landscaped gardens, the zoo houses more than 800 animals of 150 different species, including the Arabian oryx, symbol of Qatar, and indigenous feral cats, foxes, scorpions, lizards and snakes. Animals from further afield include lions, tigers, cheetahs, elephants, zebras, giraffes and ostriches. The zoo also has a small children's amusement park and a café.

To catch the best Arabian thoroughbred racehorses in action, head further along Al Furousiya Street to **Qatar Racing & Equestrian Club**, where seven races are run every Thursday from 4–7.30pm during the October to May flat-racing season. A recent addition to the racecourse is a new grandstand with seating for 1,250 and a first-floor restaurant overlooking the sand-and-turf tracks. The club is now at the centre of plans for a multi-million dollar 'race village' which aims to make it the best in the Middle East. Qatar has a long and distinguished history of breeding horses, dating at least as far back as the Umayyad era of the 7th and 8th centuries. The Al Rayyan area in which the racecourse is located has been associated with equestrian activities for generations, but professional horse-racing only took off in Qatar in the 1990s. Now, Qatar's flat-racing season is the most valuable in the world in terms of the internationally quoted owners' cost-to-prize-money ratio. The highlight of the season is the 2,400-m (12-furlong) Emir's Sword event for pure Arabians in mid-March.

While horse-racing is a regular feature on Qatar's sporting calendar, an event that has done much to elevate the city's status internationally is a massive one-off that ranks close to the Olympic Games in terms of prestige: the 2006 Asian Games. The purpose-built venue for the 15th Asian Games

Early-Rising Riders

If you can't get to a race meeting at the Racing & Equestrian Club, you can at least see the horses when they go for their daily morning gallops on the track. But you'll need to rise early: the jockeys and stable-hands are in the saddle by 5.30am, and by 7.30 the running is much less intense. At that time of day, there are so few people at the track you can strike up a conversation with a jockey or trainer. To enjoy an even closer look at the horses, wander around the nearby stables. As long as you're mindful of the notoriously jumpy high-performance horses – don't run or make any sudden moves – no one seems to mind, and the stable-hands and blacksmiths are happy to pose for photographs.

A thoroughbred at the Equestrian Club

in Doha, the first in an Arab city, is **Khalifa Sports City**, which can be reached either via Sports City Street from Salwa Road, or along Al Waab Street from D Ring Road/Al Amir Street. The cluster of impressive sports facilities, spread over 130 hectares (320 acres), can be seen for miles in the low-lying suburbs, but the most impressive by far is the landmark, 40,000-seat Khalifa Stadium, the venue for the track-and-field finals, which is characterised by a steel lighting arch that spans the length of the arena, rising to 80m (262 ft) above the field of play.

Also impressive architecturally is the nearby Aquatic Centre, Sports Hall and the Aspire Academy for Sports Excellence, which seeks to produce high-calibre sportsmen and women to represent Qatar on the world stage long after the Asian Games have moved on. Happily, there's a good foundation on which to build: with a haul of 17 medals, Qatar led the overall medal tally for Gulf Cooperation

Khalifa Sports City

Council countries at the 2002 Busan Asian Games, and its national football team lifted the Arabian Gulf Cup for the first time in 12 years in 2004. A Qatari woman, Nada Zeidan, is the leading female rally driver in the Gulf.

Not to be confused with Khalifa Sports City, **Al Sadd Stadium** on Al Waab Street is home to one of the top football teams in the Qatar National League. Al Sadd's star signings have included 1998 French World Cup winner Franc Lebœuf, one of the 'foreign legion' of international stars who have played for Qatar clubs. Lebœuf's compatriot Marcel Desailly, the former France and Chelsea captain, joined the Al Gharrafa Club, also in the western suburbs, in 2004, opting for Doha over London and Barcelona. Other famous names playing in the 2005 season included Argentina's Gabriel Batistuta and former Holland international Frank de Boer. The football season runs from October to June. In more modest surroundings, **Doha Rugby Union Club**, established in 1974, can be found between Al Sadd Stadium and Doha College on Al Bustan Street. The club welcomes rugby-orientated visitors, and its clubhouse bar is the heart of a lively social scene.

On Al Waab Street west of Khalifa Sports City are two more of Doha's large modern malls. A giant shopping trolley identifies **Hyatt Plaza**, but it is the Italian-themed **Le Villaggio** close by that's more likely to grab your attention. Opened in late 2005, Le Villaggio has a total built-up area of 145,000 sq m (1.5 million sq ft), making it the largest shopping centre in Qatar. From the outside, it's designed to look like an Italian hill town in form, scale, materials and colour. Inside, as well as a mix of major retail outlets and restaurant areas, its entertainment offerings include an ice rink, bowling alley, a six-screen cinema and fun park with roller-coaster. At the centre of the mall is an evocative coliseum. Continuing the Italian theme, its various retail, food and entertainment elements are linked by 'streets' and water features, such as an indoor canal and lake.

Confirming that you don't have to be in West Bay to find innovative architecture in Doha, the city's Al Rayyan suburb west of D Ring Road/Al Amir Street/Al Shamal (North) Road is home to Arata Isozaki's highly acclaimed **Weill Cornell Medical College-Qatar** at Education City. Isozaki's design blends themes from Arabian decorative arts and traditional Gulf buildings with modern materials to

Arata Isozaki's Weill Cornell Medical College-Qatar

create an apparently simple yet architecturally stunning structure. Geometric shapes, recalling the heritage of Islamic mathematics, are found throughout the building, in particular in the unusual three-dimensional forms of its lecture halls and the patterns on exterior walls. The lecture halls, visible between the college's North and South wings, vary in shape from ovoid to 12-sided and 20-sided, and are complemented by the main building's narrow, elongated wind-towers that are dazzling white against the uniformly blue Gulf sky. While the science and terminology associated with the structure can be baffling, the effect is simply pleasing to the eye.

Isozaki's college can be seen from Huwar Street, which is a continuation of Al Furousiya Street from Qatar Racing & Equestrian Club, but the guards at Education City's main gate seem quite happy to grant visitor passes to people who want to learn more about what the 'city' has to offer. The 7 million-sq m (75.3 million-sq ft) site, due for completion in 2008, is also home to the Qatar Foundation for Education, Science and Community Development, Carnegie Mellon Qatar, the Qatar campus of Virginia Commonwealth University (VCU) and the Texas A&M University of Qatar. It's also the venue for the monthly Doha Debates, which are broadcast across the globe on BBC World. From West Bay, Education City can be reached along Khalifa Street/Al Luqta Street from the Khalifa Tennis & Squash Complex. It's on the main road from Doha to Dukhan.

EXCURSIONS FROM DOHA

Al Wakra

Also south of Doha, on the road to Mesaieed and the Inland Sea, is the fishing and former pearling village of **Al Wakra**, now a small town of around 30,000 people. Just

Ready for renovation at Al Wakra

17km (10 miles) from the capital, Al Wakra can easily be seen in half a day or less. The most attractive feature of the town is its historic harbour, which is still the centre of a thriving local fishing industry. As at the Fishing Harbour on Doha Corniche, the timeless dhows are tied side by side along the **harbour** wall for much of the day, because fishing is done at night. But there's usually some sort of activity to be seen from the quay during the day, such as the mending of nets or engine repairs. You'll certainly be able to study the workmanship of the wood and fibreglass boats up close.

A curious feature of dhows is the waist-high open-topped wooden box strapped near the stern: it serves as the fishermen's bathroom, shower and toilet.

Away from the quay, situated in the shallow waters around the harbour, the low walls of limestone that look like mazes are inter-tidal

An Al Wakra mosque and houses

fishing traps, known locally as *maskar*. The nearby sandy **beach** is one of the most popular public beaches in the country.

Al Wakra is also well known throughout Qatar for its fine **mosques**, the few old **Islamic-style houses** that have survived the ravages of the Gulf climate, and for its small **museum** (open Sun–Fri 8am–noon and 3–6pm), which has an exhibition of traditional doors and other displays on architecture and natural history, in particular life under the sea, with which the town is so closely associated.

Umm Salal Mohammed

North of Doha, some 20km (12 miles) from the centre of the city, but only 9km (5½ miles) along Route 1 from Landmark Shopping Mall, the village of **Umm Salal Mohammed** provides a glimpse of how life was lived away from the coast. Its most famous landmark, **Barzan Tower** (opening times vary), can be seen from the main road linking the capital with Qatar's northern towns, 2km (1 mile) east of the village.

Built in the late 19th century in a style that's unique in the Gulf, the three-storey, rectangular-shaped fortification with external staircase is actually the western watchtower of two defensive structures standing at the edge of the present-day village. Both towers have recently been restored.

Some 1.5km (1 mile) further into the village, along Mohd Bin Jasim Street, **Umm Salal Mohammed Fort** is distinguishable by its high thick walls and imposing façade. Constructed in the late 19th century as a residential fort for Sheikh Jassim Bin Mohammad, it's badly in need of the attention given to Barzan Tower if its grandeur is to be preserved. With no opening hours as such, visitors may have to make do with seeing the fort from the outside, but that alone is worthwhile.

Continuing through the village, during the cooler winter months you can find rest and refreshment – tea or coffee and dates – in the Bedouin-style surroundings of the Al Khima Restaurant, a large, open-sided tent located on open ground at the northern edge of the village.

Back on Route 1, 7km (4 miles) north of Umm Salal Mohammed is the impressively tidy village of Umm Salal Ali. On its northern boundary are ancient burial mounds that are believed to date back to the 3rd millennium BC.

Umm Salal Mohammed Fort

Al Khor

Visitors have been leaving their mark in the quiet but historic port of Al Khor since the Stone Age. Archaeological finds of pottery here suggest the area had links with the pre-Sumerian Ubaid civilisation, which existed in southern Mesopotamia between 5600 and 3900BC. Further finds on two nearby islands show that inhabitants of Dilmun – present-day Bahrain – brought their Barbar pottery and stone fireplaces to Al Khor in the Bronze Age, around 2000BC. 'Why the people at this site came to Al Khor is unclear,' says an exhibit at the town's museum. Happily, the reasons you've come here will be as clear as the waters in Al Khor bay: there's a harbour, museum and mangrove plantation to see.

Al Khor, known in history as Al Shaqiq, was once a centre for Qatar's thriving pearl trade, but after the double whammy of the Wall Street Crash and the Japanese invention of

Al Khor, a former pearl-fishing port

the cultured pearl in the 1930s, the bottom dropped out of the market in almost no time, and the port's importance waned. That said, there's still life in the old **harbour** today: as at Al Wakra south of Doha, the quay is home to a flotilla of traditional dhows that ply the ancient fishing grounds. The distinctive vessels, many of which proudly fly the Qatar national flag, can be inspected at close range along the quay.

Up to the 1930s, in the pearling season between May and September, the pearling dhows of Qatar's great trading families would have sailed from here to the offshore beds where the pearl oysters were plentiful, but the only pearling dhow to be seen today is displayed onshore, near one of the town's several surviving **watchtowers** on the Corniche.

The story of Al Khor and the region around is explained in **Al Khor Museum** (open Sun–Thur 8am–noon and 3–6pm, Fri 8am–noon, Sat 3–6pm). The small fortress-like building, a former police station, is at the harbour end of the Corniche. As well as displaying the evidence of Barbar visitation, an exhibit details Babylonian interest in Al Khor between 1300 and 1200BC. 'These Babylonians seem to have been attracted to Al Khor to make a purple dye from a certain kind of marine shellfish,' the exhibit explains. 'This dye, which was used to colour wool clothing, is also called Tyrian or royal purple, and was used to make highly prestigious and very expensive garments for Babylonian kings.'

North of the town, the **mangrove plantation** at Al Thakhirah offers a rare splash of natural greenery along an otherwise barren coastline. A haven for various species of birds, it's a popular spot among ornithologists in Qatar.

Though rather sleepy today, Al Khor is due a facelift under Qatar Tourism Authority's plans to add more beach resorts to the country's coastline. The Al Fareej Resort is to occupy a sandy spit to the south of the bay. An attractively landscaped resort village for families, it will have Arabian-style chalets and will be dotted with watchtowers, just like the old town itself.

Al Khor can be reached by one of two routes from Doha: the more direct Al Jamiaa Street past the Qatar University campus and Doha Golf Club – Route 14, along which you'll see the 5.6-km (3.4-mile) long Lusail International Circuit, the MotoGP venue some 21km (13 miles) from West Bay's City Center mall – or via Route 1 past Umm Salal Mohammed. At around 17km (10 miles) after Umm Salal Ali you will need to turn right for Al Khor. The distance from City Center mall to Al Khor's dhow harbour is just 47km (29 miles), so a visit can be done in half a day from the capital. Alternatively, you can combine a trip to Al Khor with other sights further north and west.

Jebel Jassasiya

The most significant site for stone carvings in Qatar is at Jebel Jassasiya, a rocky ridge between the coastal communities of Huwailah and Fuwairit in the northeast of the peninsula. Notoriously difficult to find if you're not on an organised tour, the 900 carvings, first catalogued in 1974, are believed to date back to prehistoric times, though their

Porcelain and Pearls

South of Jebel Jassasiya, the rural backwater of Huwailah was one of the main urban centres on the Qatar Peninsula in the 18th century. Remains of buildings show that the town stretched for 2km (1 mile) along the coast and had a square stone fort. Its deep bay could provide anchorage for large vessels that sailed the international trade routes from Mesopotamia and Persia to the Far East. Links with China are attested to by discoveries here of Chinese porcelain fragments dating back to the mid-17th century. Pearl fishing was a key activity until the town was destroyed in an internal war in 1835.

exact origin is unknown. As well as simple engraved images of various kinds of boats, there are rows of small holes of the type used in two traditional Arabic games with stone counters: *al aailah* and *al haloosah.*

North of Jebel Jassasiya, **Fuwairit** was a base for the ruling Al-Thani family before they moved to Al Bida (Doha) in 1847. The birthplace of Sheikh Mohammad Bin Thani, the town is known for its public beach.

THE INLAND SEA

One of the great natural wonders of the Arabian Gulf lies less than two hours to the south of Doha: **Khor Al Udaid,** more commonly known as the Inland Sea. Located in the far southeast of the country, adjacent to the Qatar Peninsula's 60-km (37-mile) land border with Saudi Arabia, the Inland Sea is not, as its name in English would suggest, a land-

The Inland Sea

Making desert tracks

places thick with seagrass, are the habitat of the endangered dugong, or sea cow, an ancient species of herbivorous marine mammal that's believed to have given rise to the mermaid legend among sailors. But during weekends, the only 'wild' life you're likely to see are Toyotas, Nissans and Land-Rovers performing the terrestrial equivalent of aerobatics across the imposing walls of sand.

Undoubtedly one of the most scenic areas of Qatar, the Inland Sea is being put forward by the government of Qatar as a possible UNESCO Natural World Heritage Site, a status that would place it on a par with Australia's Great Barrier Reef and America's Grand Canyon. At the very least, the Inland Sea is likely to designated as one of several new national parks by the government.

If you're part of an organised tour, it's possible to stay overnight in the dunes south of the **Sealine Beach Resort**, where there's a tour-company camp with Bedouin-style hospitality tents that's an atmospheric venue for campfire suppers and Arabian-themed entertainment. One of the benefits of an overnight stay in the desert is that you can see both sunset and sunrise, and so better appreciate how the light can dramatically alter the appearance of the landscape at different times of day. If you are overnighting in the desert, do carry warm clothes – the temperatures can drop significantly at night, even in summer. The camp is just a stone's throw from the sandy shoreline of the Arabian Gulf, so you can look forward to a refreshing morning swim, but the oil-related industry up the coast in Mesaieed is an ugly blot on the landscape. At the camp you'll also have an opportunity to experience sand-skiing or sand-boarding. It's a short but exciting ride down a dune. The sand cushions even the hardest of falls, but if you're about to wipe out, remember to close your mouth.

Just north of the campsite, a comfortable night's sleep is guaranteed at the Sealine Beach Resort, a popular weekend destination for Doha's resident expats. Managed by Qatar National Hotels Company (QNHC), the resort is set among well-established gardens that are a haven for birdlife and butterflies. It has an Olympic-size swimming pool, a separate lagoon-style pool and a water-sports centre where you can rent windsurfing boards and jet-skis. For land-based excitement, quad bikes are available for racing along the sand, and there are pony and camel rides for all age groups. The resort also has a children's playground. Day visitors are welcome to use the resort's facilities for a reasonable fee.

Sand-skiing

QATAR'S FORTS

Al Zubara

Qatar has older forts, but none is more impressively located than **Al Zubara** (open daily 6.30am–6pm), in the northwest of the country, 105km (65 miles) from Doha. The fort is visible from at least 5km (3 miles) away as you approach Al Zubara on the secondary road from Route 1. It's the only building in an otherwise featureless landscape. Located on a slight rise some 2km (1 mile) from the Arabian Gulf, it overlooks the ruins of the much older town of Al Zubara.

Built in 1938 during the reign of Sheikh Abdullah Bin Jassim Al-Thani, the ochre-coloured fort is square-shaped with a single inner courtyard, circular towers on three of its corners and a rectangular tower on the fourth. Because of the simplicity of its design and the basic materials used in its construction – mud bricks and coral stones with gypsum plaster and mortar – it looks far more ancient than it actually is, but was used by the Qatar military as recently as the 1980s. The fort has served as a coastguard station

The Ottomans' Eastern Port

In the 18th century, Al Zubara, already an established pearling port, became the Bani Khalid's regional headquarters – and also the Ottomans' principal transit port for their eastern and central Arabian territories. From Surat in India came fabrics, bamboo, coffee, sugar, pepper, spices, tin, oil, ghee and rice, all loaded onto camels at Al Zubara, bound for the Arabian interior. It was from Al Zubara that Qatar was ruled by the Al-Khalifa clan of the central Arabian Utub tribe, who had lived in Kuwait under the suzerainty of the Bani Khalid. Today, the Al-Khalifas are the rulers of Bahrain.

Al Zubara Fort, built in 1938

and a base for the country's Frontier Army. Restored in 1987, it's now a regional museum, though its few dusty exhibits are no match for the appeal of the building itself. Its bleak, isolated location and few neighbouring palm trees give it the air of a lonely desert outpost in a French Foreign Legion adventure.

Between the fort and the sea, excavations have uncovered the foundations of the walled city of **Al Zubara**, which has been preserved as Alzubara Heritage Site by the Museums and Antiquities Department of the National Council for Culture, Arts & Heritage. Picking your way between the crumbled coral-stone walls, crunching over a desert floor covered with tiny seashells, it's hard to believe that less than 250 years ago this was the thriving capital of Qatar, the regional administrative headquarters for the Bani Khalid overlords of Kuwait, who controlled the peninsula and much of the Arabian interior.

Al Thughb

Continuing north from Al Zubara, along the road to the regional administrative centre of Madinat Al Shamal, there are more forts to see at Al Thughb and Al Rakiyat. **Al Thughb Fort** (Kalet althakb), less than 15km (9 miles) from Al Zubara, is also rectangular in shape with four corner watchtowers, a common design for desert forts constructed between the 17th and early 20th centuries. This particular fort dates back to the late 19th century. It's not visible from the main road: to reach it you should turn right just before the dusty junction to Al Areesh radio station and head along a disused road towards a patch of greenery – a farm. The fort will come into view, but at some point you will need to turn right again onto a stony track. A four-wheel-drive is preferable to a saloon car, but it's possible to get there in the latter with great care. Though in a good state of repair, the fort is

Al Thughb Fort

an empty shell and has no opening times as such: there's no door, so entry is possible at any time.

A few kilometres further north, **Al Rakiyat Fort** (Kalet alrkiat) is also off the main road. To reach it, turn right along the track that begins near the National Council for Culture, Arts & Heritage sign and continue for around 1km (½ mile). Dating from the same period as Al Thughb Fort, it has three square corners and a squat round tower on the fourth. It, too, is a shell with no restrictions on entrance. It was restored in 1988, but its walls are nevertheless crumbling in the harsh climate, revealing the various layers of materials used in the construction process.

Al Wajbah

West of Doha, 15km (9.3 miles) from the city in Al Rayyan, the town of **Al Wajbah** is home to the ruler's main palace and one of Qatar's oldest forts, both of which are depicted on the country's 500 Riyal note. While you'd have to be a head of state to see inside the ruler's palace, sumptuously decorated by Assimo Dalla Torre architects of Rome, **Al Wajbah Fort** is undergoing restoration to welcome visitors. It was built in 1882, and in 1893 its towers and thick walls witnessed a famous battle in which Qatari fighters, led by the then ruler, Sheikh Jassim Bin Mohammad Bin Thani, 'the founder of modern Qatar', defeated the forces of the mighty Ottoman Empire. Al Wajbah lies just south of the main road from Doha to Dukhan (Route 3). To reach it, take the first left after the Al Wajbah roundabout.

Al Samariyah

Also south of the Doha–Dukhan road, 40km (25 miles) from the capital, the farming community of Al Samariyah is home to one of Qatar's more unusual museums, the **Faisal Bin Qassim Al-Thani Museum** (tel: 522 0530; opening times vary), which houses the eponymous sheikh's private collection of Islamic arms and armour, ceramics, glasswork and metalwork, coins, fossils, textiles and embroidery, and classic cars. In all, 3,000 pieces collected over nearly half a century have been gathered in a recently constructed building that's a combination of fortress and palace. The sheikh's lush, densely wooded farm, inhabited by numerous peacocks and peahens, is just behind the museum.

AL SHAHANIYA

The small town of Al Shahaniya, 2km (1 mile) along the Dukhan road from Al Samariyah, is worth visiting for two unique attractions: it has Qatar's main camel racetrack and the Al Maha Sanctuary, a breeding centre and reserve for Qatar's national symbol, the Arabian oryx.

➤ The **Al Shahaniya Camel Racetrack**, 4km (2½ miles) north of the Doha–Dukhan road, not only offers visitors a rare opportunity to witness one of the sporting world's more unusual spectacles – a racing camel can reach a top speed of around 40kph (25mph) – but also recalls a bygone age when

Bring on the Robot Jockeys

Camel races are tough tests of endurance around tracks that vary in length between 6 and 10km (3½–6 miles). Although betting is not allowed, tension on race day is heightened by corporate-sponsored prize money of hundreds of thousands of dollars. The sport has been criticised by human rights groups in the West for its use of small boys as jockeys, but the Qatar government has invested more than $1.3 million to develop alternative, robot jockeys – Swiss-designed titanium devices that look like small humans with whips. Robot jockeys were successfully tested at Al Shahaniya in 2005 and are due to be fully introduced by 2007.

Exercising on the camel racetrack at Al Shahaniya

camels were the main form of transport across the desert sands. One of the highlights of the season, which runs from October to May, is the HH the Emir's Camel Race for GCC Countries, which has been held annually since 1973 and sees various breeds of camels, Arabian, Omani and Sudanese, competing for the title Champion of Champions.

During the racing season, tour companies arrange visits to Al Shahaniya according to the race schedule – either very early in the morning or in the late afternoon. But if you can't get there on race day, don't worry: you can still see camels during their daily practice runs. The best time to get to the track is between 7–9am or 3.30–5pm, when the road behind the grandstand is crossed by so many camel trains heading to and from the surrounding stables you won't know which way to point your camera.

If you have a car, drive towards the front of the grandstand and do your own loop of the course: a road runs inside the rails enabling you to follow the camels around the track. The shops near by are geared to meeting the needs of breeders, owners and trainers rather than tourists, but you'll find inexpensive camel blankets in them, and a supermarket with snacks and cold drinks.

Al Maha Sanctuary

Another of Qatar's iconic desert dwellers can be seen at close range at the **Al Maha Sanctuary** in Al Shahaniya, near the Doha–Dukhan road. Once threatened with extinction, the Arabian oryx – *al maha* in Arabic – is now bred in protected herds here. A permit from the Ministry of Municipal Affairs and Agriculture is required to get into the sanctuary, so it's recommended you go with a tour operator who will take care of the red tape (*see Travel Tips, page 122*). Alternatively, you can see Arabian oryx at Doha zoo.

Arabian oryx in Al Maha Sanctuary

ZIKREET

The town of Zikreet

A favourite camping destination among expat residents, **Zikreet** lies at the neck of a narrow peninsula that juts into the Arabian Gulf north of the oil town of Dukhan on Qatar's west coast. Zikreet is best-known for the intriguing shapes and overhangs that the wind has carved out of the soft sedimentary rock of its **limestone ridges**. To appreciate them best, you'll need to turn off Route 3 some 8km (5 miles) short of Dukhan and head towards Zikreet village. Before the village, around 2km (1 mile) from the Route 3 turn-off, take a dirt track to the right that follows a low boundary wall. One of the most striking outcrops, resembling a giant mushroom, will soon come into view. It's possible to reach it in a normal car if you drive very carefully over the gravel and stones, but a four-wheel-drive is recommended.

Zikreet village itself has an interesting little **mosque**. On the far side of the village, at the Kalet zekret archaeological site, the foundations of one of the west coast's many old fortresses have been unearthed. A series of channels carved into the floor on the seaside of the fortress are what's left of a date press – the juice being squeezed into the grooves and collected.

South of Zikreet, Dukhan is where oil, or 'black gold', was first discovered in Qatar in 1940. It's mentioned on tourist maps, but there's really nothing of interest there. The oil-industry town has a gated entrance that prevents outsiders from venturing in. Outside its walls, Dukhan Water Sports Club on the near by shoreline is strictly for members only.

On the Water

There are few more memorable places in the Gulf for a swim than Qatar's Inland Sea, but hotel swimming pools are generally safer, more relaxing alternatives to the Arabian Gulf.

The crystal-clear, warm waters of the Arabian Gulf offer great diving opportunities for experienced sub-aqua enthusiasts. The tour company Gulf Adventures (tel: 431 5555) offers a three-day Drive and Dive package. Qatar International Tours (QIT) (tel: 466 7782) organises instructor-accompanied tours to a coral reef. Equipment and lunch is provided, but the minimum number for a trip is 15. For beginners, equipment hire and tuition are available at Pearl Divers (tel: 444 9553), Coral Diving School (tel: 466 1434) and Doha Sub-Aqua Club (tel: 565 1775).

The Regatta Sailing Academy at the Sheraton Hotel (tel: 550 7846) offers lessons in dinghy sailing, yachting and windsurfing by British-qualified instructors. Most beachfront hotels, such as the Sheraton and InterContinental in Doha and

Trips in Boats

It's possible to organise your own **dhow trip** on a traditional fishing vessel: from around 4pm each day they can be found on Doha Corniche at the jetty near the Sheraton Hotel or near the Balhambar Restaurant. But for a little extra sparkle – an on-board barbecue, a visit to an outlying island or the chance for a moonlight swim – consider going with a tour company.

A full-day, tour-company-organised **fishing trip** on a traditional dhow or modern fishing boat gives visitors the opportunity to reel in barracuda, kingfish and perhaps swordfish, among many other Gulf species. Equipment is provided. The InterFitness Club at the InterContinental Hotel (tel: 484 4979) also offers fishing trips: boats can be hired by the day or half-day.

A spot of golf

the Sealine Beach Resort south of Mesaieed, have watersports centres offering jet-skiing and windsurfing. There are also opportunities to water-ski and parasail in Qatar.

Golf

Non-members are welcome to play the world-class 18-hole Championship Course at Doha Golf Club (tel: 483 2338), the venue for the Qatar Masters. Alternatively, you can try the less challenging nine-hole floodlit Academy Course. Golf clubs are available for hire and qualified PGA pros offer lessons for adults and juniors.

Other Activities

Unlikely as it may seem, there's an **ice rink** at Winter Wonderland at City Center. The centrepiece of the mall's main atrium, it's open year-round. There's a fee for the novelty of learning how to skate in one of the hottest countries on earth, but more limited coaching is provided free of charge. The 32-lane **Qatar Bowling Centre** (tel: 444 3355), near the junction of B Ring Road and Al Rayyan Road in Rumeila, is the place for competitive ten-pin bowling. Winter Wonderland (tel: 483 9501) at the City Center mall has eight lanes.

SPECTATOR SPORTS

Tennis

The biggest names in men's tennis compete in the week-long $1-million ATP Qatar Open held at the Khalifa Tennis & Squash Complex in Doha every January. The following month, the stars of the women's game grace the same courts in the $600,000 WTA Qatar Open for Women. In April, the male stars of yesteryear compete in the ATP Champions Tour event.

Golf

The annual $1.5-million Qatar Masters takes place at Doha Golf Club in West Bay in January, and attracts many of the world's top golfers. Among its former champions is Ernie Els, who won in 2005.

Horse-racing

Qatar is known throughout the world for the quality of its Arabian thoroughbreds. The flat racing season at Qatar Racing & Equestrian Club, in Al Rayyan, Doha, runs from October to May. Races are held each Thursday from 4–7.30pm: free admission, betting strictly forbidden. The 2,400-m (12-furlong) Emir's Sword race for pure Arabians in March is the highlight of the season. The club is also the venue for an annual international show jumping event in February/March.

Camel-racing

The 'Sport of Sheikhs' can be watched between October and May at the Al Shahaniya Camel Racetrack *(see page 78)*. The highlight of the season is the annual HH The Emir Camel Race for GCC Countries every April, in which Arabian, Omani and Sudanese camels compete for total prize money of around $800,000 and the title Champion of Champions. Tour companies arrange visits.

Motorsport

The world-class 5.6-km (3.4-mile) Losail International Circuit, 25km (15 miles) north of central Doha, hosts the annual Qatar round of the World Superbike Championship in February and the Qatar MotoGP Grand Prix every September/October. In April, Qatar's desert terrain is the setting for the annual Qatar International Rally, round four of the FIA's

Qatar International Rally

A Qatar regatta

Middle East Rally Championship for cars.

Football

Qataris are passionate about football and their National League is one of the best in the Middle East, with top international players, including Brazil's Romario, Argentina's Gabriel Batistuta and France's Marcel Desailly playing or having played for its clubs. Among the top local teams are Al Sadd, Al Gharrafa, Al Rayyan and Al Arabi. Matches are held on weekday evenings as well as on weekends (Thursday and Friday) between October and June. The highlights of the season are the National League play-offs in April, the Heir Apparent's Cup in April/May and the Emir's Cup in May/June.

Water Sports

Three traditional sailing events evoke Qatar's seafaring heritage. HH the Prime Minister's Championship for Traditional Sailing Boats in February is followed by HH the Heir Apparent's Championship in March and HH the Emir's Championship in April. Meanwhile, the Qatar International Sailing Championship takes place each February. An altogether noisier water-sport is held in Doha Bay every October/November: the Qatar round of the UIM Class I World Powerboat Championship.

Other Sports

Qatar's prominence in world sport was given a huge boost by the awarding of the 2006 Asian Games to Doha, which has been the catalyst for the development of world-class facilities, such as the 40,000-seat Khalifa Stadium in Doha. The world's top cyclists compete in the Tour of Qatar road race in January/February, and its top fencers face off in the Qatar International Fencing Championship in January.

Sport on TV

If you need to know how your local team are getting on, international football, rugby, cricket and Formula 1 racing are shown on the big screen TV at Aussie Legends sports bar in the Rydges Plaza Hotel, at the Shehrazad Lounge Bar & Irish Terrace in the Ramada Hotel and at Amigo's in the Khalifa Tennis & Squash Complex.

SHOPPING

With the relatively recent introduction of bright, spacious Western-style malls in Doha, shopping – or just hanging out in a mall – has grown as a recreational activity, especially in the summer months when malls are among the few places offering an outdoor-style experience in air-conditioned comfort. Malls are generally open 10am–10pm on weekdays (Sat–Thur), and 3–10pm on Fridays, the local weekend. However, for most visitors a visit to Doha's more traditional *souqs* will take priority. Prices aren't

Inside the Shopping Mall

usually fixed in *souqs*, and haggling is welcomed. They are generally open 8.30am–12.30pm and 4–8pm on weekdays (Sat–Thur), and 4–8pm on Fridays.

Bright fabrics for sale in a *souq*

Where to Buy

Souq Waqif is the oldest souq in Doha. Its atmospheric, narrow alleyways lie behind a pleasingly restored traditional frontage on Souq Waqif Street in the old city centre. Within walking distance are the more modern *souq* buildings bordered by Jasim Bin Mohammed Street, Ali Bin Abdullah Street and Jabr Bin Mohammed Street. Much less 'Arabian' on the senses than Souq Waqif, they include Al Jaidah Souq, Souq Al Najdada, Souq Al Ahmad, Souq Faleh, Souq Nasser Bin Saif, Souq Al Asiery, Doha Souq, Souq Al Deira and Souq Al Jabor. Though some are well known for particular items (Souq Al Asiery for inexpensive textiles, Souq Al Deira for more upmarket textiles), most have a mix of traders selling perfume, clothing, shoes, accessories, luggage, electrical items and audio tapes and CDs.

The five-storey **City Center Doha** is located in West Bay near the Sheraton and Four Seasons hotels. Its anchor stores are Debenhams and Carrefour, the French supermarket chain. **Landmark Shopping Mall**, at the junction of Al Markhiya Street and Al Shamal (North) Road, includes branches of Marks & Spencer and BHS. **The Mall**, on D Ring Road near the airport, has a smaller selection of brand-name outlets. **Le Villaggio** and **Hyatt Plaza** are both on Al Waab Street, west of Khalifa Sports City.

What to Buy

Weaving and Embroidery. From Souq Waqif: *bukhnoq* head-coverings decorated with embroidery and gold-and-silver thread, traditionally worn by Qatari girls; *thobe al nashl* dresses worn by women on special occasions; women's *sirwal* baggy trousers with embroidered tight ankle cuffs, traditionally worn under dresses; men's ceremonial lightweight *bisht* cloaks, in cream, brown or black with gold edging.

Fabrics. From Souq Al Deira: exclusive beaded fabrics, heavy lace and Western-style quality fabrics for women's clothes. Souq Al Asiery sells less expensive fabrics, from cotton to lace, for day or evening wear, sari fabric, natural and man-made fibres and modern stretch fabrics. Bombay Silk Centre on Al Kharaba Street has a colourful selection of exotic Indian and Far Eastern silk at comparatively low prices. Made-to-measure tailoring for men, women and children is available on Al Kahraba Street. Tailors can work from your own design or duplicate existing garments, for collection between two days and a week later.

Carpets. From Oriental Carpet Co., on C Ring Road: handmade carpets and rugs, including pure silk Persian carpets.

Gold. From the 'Gold Souq', a cluster of jewellery shops off Al Ahmed Street

When interacting with Qataris, don't give or receive items with your left hand – it's associated with ablutions. And sitting in a way that displays the soles of your feet or shoes is considered rude in Qatar.

Bedouin women would traditionally collect jewellery as insurance against hard times. On their death, it was melted down and re-worked because custom forbade young brides from wearing dead women's jewellery.

and Ali Bin Abdullah Street: 22-carat gold necklaces, bangles and brooches, locally made bridal jewellery, Bedouin jewellery (ask, as it's not always displayed).

Perfume. From Souq Waqif: blends of essential oils from perfume vendors. Also head for Ajmal in City Center mall.

Incense. From Souq Waqif and Omani Market: sweet-smelling *oudh*, traditionally burnt as a sign of hospitality; frankincense from Oman; *bokhur* – a mix of *oudh*, white musk, sandalwood oil, ambergris, mystica and rose oil; and brass, ceramic or wood incense-burners.

Spices. From Souq Waqif: for cooking or display (the traders will fill your own glass containers with layers of differently coloured ground spices).

Other. *Shisha* water pipes, sold in their own carry cases; traditional coffee pots and cups; camel blankets.

ENTERTAINMENT

Nightlife

Not so long ago the Sheraton Hotel was the only place in Doha where alcohol was served. Now, alcohol is widely available in hotel bars and restaurants throughout the city, even in the minibars of rooms. However, there are no bars outside hotels or clubs, and alcohol isn't served in street cafés and restaurants – the notable exception being Amigo's at the Khalifa Tennis & Squash Complex. So don't expect beer or wine at Ramada Junction's trendy cafés. On the plus side, many of the venues that do serve alcohol remain open until the small hours. visitors should note that alcohol is not served at all during the Muslim holy month of Ramadan.

For lively, casual bars in the city centre, head to Amigo's, Aussie Legends at the Rydges Plaza Hotel or the Shehrazad Lounge Bar and Irish Terrace at the Ramada Hotel. Out of town, Paloma at the InterContinental Hotel has an informal Tex-Mex atmosphere and transforms into a nightclub from midnight each day. For those in search of a more sophisticated cocktail-bar experience, The Library on the top floor of the Ramada and Piano Piano jazz lounge at the Mövenpick Hotel are two city-centre options, while the Admiral's Club at The Ritz-Carlton Hotel and Spikes Lounge at Doha Golf Club are out of town.

Many bars have a dance floor, but Doha's main nightclub is the Cloudnyn discothèque on the mezzanine floor of the

Doha dazzles at night

Musicians at a local festival

Al Sadd Merweb Hotel, at the intersection of C Ring Road and Al Sadd Street. The resident DJ is on from 10.30pm daily. Entry is restricted to couples, but single in-house guests are welcome. There is a dress code.

For a typically Arabian night out, head for a venue where *shisha* water pipes, or ‘hubbly-bubbly’, are served. The most popular is the *shisha* tent at the Al Bustan Hotel, near Qatar National Museum on Al Muthaf Street. Al Layali in Souq Najd is a highly rated upmarket alternative. On the Corniche, *shisha* is served at the Balhambar and Al Bandar restaurants, at the Al Jawhara Gallery in the Ras al Nasaa complex and at the Marina Café in the Doha Club. Out of town, Shisha Diwan at The Ritz-Carlton offers a more formal dining environment with *shisha.* To see belly-dancing, book a night out at the Al Shaheen Restaurant at the Sheraton, where there are two shows nightly, at 10.45pm and midnight.

Live Music

Amigo's, Shehrazad, Paloma, The Library and Piano Piano have live music by Western or Asian performers most evenings from around 8pm. During the cooler months, The Ritz-Carlton hosts Music Under The Stars at its poolside Flamingos restaurant on the second Thursday of the month, and Jazz Under The Stars on the fourth Thursday. Every afternoon, a classical trio or harpist accompanies afternoon tea in the Ritz-Carlton's Lobby Lounge. The hotel's open-air theatre is the setting for concerts by international stars such as Lionel Ritchie, who performed there in 2004. Take note, there are no live music performances during the Muslim holy month of Ramadan.

Performing Arts

The annual Doha Festival of Arts and Culture, also known as Doha Cultural Festival, in March, brings international productions to Qatar. Luciano Pavarotti sang there during the 2003 event. World-class performers also appear during the annual Summer Wonders Festival of Fun, between June and August. Recent visitors include a Russian ballet company and flamenco dancers from Spain. On public holidays, such as National Day on 3 September and the Muslim Eid festivals, traditional song-and-dance groups and the Qatari Armed Forces Military Band can be found in parks and other public venues.

Top-class shows take place

Cinema and Television

There are multi-screen cinemas in all the major malls, but if you're hoping to see

EATING OUT

Foreigners have been trading in and through Qatar for thousands of years, so it should come as no surprise to anyone lifting the lid on this historic entrepôt that simmering within there's a heady mix of international cuisines. French, Italian, Indian, Chinese, Japanese – the great cuisines of the world have been welcomed by an indigenous population with broad international tastes.

Historically, the inhabitants of the peninsula lived off fish, lamb from Bedouin flocks and, occasionally, camel meat. Today, much of the locally caught fish and meat goes into Lebanese, European and Far Eastern dishes in the capital's restaurants, but it's still possible to sample traditional Qatari fare, such as seafood served with delicately seasoned rice, and simple, Bedouin-style *matchbous* (spiced lamb with rice) and *hareis* (slow-cooked wheat and lamb).

For Arabic cuisine in general, however, read Lebanese. Entrepreneurial travellers since the days of their Phoenician ancestors, the Lebanese have brought a distinctly Mediterranean flavour to Arabian food, with liberal amounts of lemon, olive oil, thyme, parsley and mint in dishes, and hot and cold *mezze* – similar to Spanish tapas – bringing a welcome variety to meals.

Meal Times

Meal times are typical for an international business destination: breakfast from around 6.30am to 9am, lunch between 1pm and 3pm and dinner not earlier than 8pm. Traditionally, lunch is the main meal in the day for Qataris, who take an extended lunch break-cum-siesta between noon and 3.30pm.

Not all hotel restaurants open for lunch, but those that do are generally open from noon to 3pm. In the evening, opening

Pulses and spices in the market

times vary between 6.30 and 7.30, and closing times between 11 and midnight. On the street, Arabic, Indian and Pakistani outlets, Western-style casual-dining restaurants and stylish cafés tend to remain open throughout the day, while the food courts in shopping malls keep mall hours.

Probably the most sociable meal in a normal week is the all-you-can-eat Friday brunch, an extended international buffet at a hotel that's enjoyed by locals and resident ex-pats alike. Generally, Friday brunches are from around noon to 3.30 or 4pm. Popular venues include The Lagoon Restaurant at the Ritz-Carlton and Amwaj at the InterContinental. Most hotels provide special activities to keep children entertained.

WHERE TO EAT

Eating out in Qatar is generally done in one of four places: at a hotel, at a club, in a street venue or in shopping malls. If you want to enjoy alcohol with your meal, your choice is immediately restricted to hotels and clubs.

Hotels

Hotel restaurants cater for the wider community, so you needn't be concerned about being artificially cocooned from daily life if you eat at a hotel. In fact, some of Qatar's most popular venues are in its five-star hotels, and to guarantee yourself a table you may need to book in advance.

The top fine-dining restaurants include Al Shaheen at the Sheraton, which offers an international menu with a tilt towards Arabic, and La Mer, the French restaurant at the Ritz-Carlton. Both offer fabulous views of the Arabian Gulf. There are several classic French and Italian restaurants to choose from – Maxim at the Ramada, Il Teatro at the Four Seasons and Porcini at the Ritz-Carlton – but more casual-themed restaurants are gaining in popularity: two hotel Tex-Mex restaurants are Paloma at the InterContinental and Salsa at the Marriott.

Fast Food

The one time of year when the daily routine of meal-times alters dramatically is during Ramadan, the month when Muslims fast during daylight hours. During Ramadan, even non-Muslims aren't permitted to eat or drink in public. Accordingly, all non-hotel restaurants are closed until sunset. During the day, it is possible to eat in hotel restaurants that are shielded from view behind wooden screens.

Once the sun has dipped below the horizon, there's a festival atmosphere until the early hours, with much feasting and fun. Most restaurants will have elaborate *Iftar*, or break-fast, buffets of traditional Arabic food that people of all faiths are welcome to share.

No alcohol is served during Ramadan.

The choice is yours, at the Balhambar restaurant

Za Moda, at the InterContinental, gives a stylish and contemporary twist to Italian pasta dishes. For sushi, sashimi, tempura and teppanyaki, there's Sakura at the Ramada and Asia Live! in the Marriott. Options for Indian food in hotels include Chingari at the Ramada and Taj Rasoi at the Marriott. The place for locally caught seafood is the InterContinental's Sultan Ibrahim fish restaurant.

Clubs

The restaurants in Doha's various private clubs are open to non-members. Fine-dining opportunities include Al-Sayyad at the Diplomatic Club near the Ritz-Carlton. The club also has a steakhouse, Le Grill. The Dana Club, alongside the Khalifa Tennis & Squash Complex, offers an international menu, including Arabic dishes, at its Lewan restaurant. At the Doha Club, near the Marriott, the first-floor Al Dar offers an extensive Arabic and Asian menu.

Chef with a plate of sweets at Café Batteel, Doha

On the Street

The terraces of the few restaurants on Doha Corniche are among the most pleasant places to eat during the cooler months. The Balhambar Restaurant specialises in Qatari cuisine. Typical appetisers include *jarjir* (rocca leaves and onion), *roub* (cucumber with yoghurt), *nakhi* (boiled chickpeas) and *bajella* (boiled *foul*, a black-bean stew). Main dishes include grilled lamb and chicken, lamb chops and seafood, including *hammour* (a Gulf species of grouper), kingfish and shrimps. Simple deserts include *mehalabiya* (milk custard with pistachios and rose water) and *logaimat* (fried balls made from egg, flour and saffron).

More mainstream Lebanese fare is available at Al Sharqi, in the Al Bandar group of restaurants near the Fishing Harbour, and at Al Jawhara Gallery in the Ras Al Nasaa complex at the southern end of the Corniche. Probably the best Lebanese restaurant in Doha, however, is Al Layali, on Salwa Road, near Ramada Junction. For a more workaday atmosphere, Barbar Lebanese Fast Food, at Ramada Junction, does sit in and takeaway meals (sandwiches) daily 5pm–1am.

For budget-conscious travellers, there are numerous small restaurants throughout Doha selling delicious and filling Arabic sandwiches of *shawarma* (grilled lamb or chicken sliced from a spit) and falafel for tiny outlays of riyals. Turkey Central Restaurant on Al Merqab Street offers excellent-value-for-money regional dishes, including hummus, *moutabbal* (grilled aubergine, *tahini* and lemon paste) and *tabouleh* (chopped parsley salad with mint, fresh tomatoes, onion and crushed wheat), grilled meats and *fatayer* (pastry pies). There are also a great many restaurants selling cheap and delicious Indian and Pakistani dishes. One of the best south Indian restaurants is The Garden on Al Kahraba Street, which serves up *dosa* and *idly* for breakfast from 7am. For north Indian food in a more formal restaurant atmosphere, head for Bukhara at the Khalifa Tennis & Squash Complex.

The best-value Thai restaurant is the unpretentious Thai Noodles, opposite Souq Al Asiery in the Grand Hamad Street area, which is open daily 8am–11pm. Along with the usual red and green curries and stir-fried dishes, conventional taste buds are accommodated with chicken nuggets *(Gai Nuggets Tod)* and hotdog with fried rice and vegetables *(Kao Phad Hotdog)*. A favourite Chinese restaurant for lunch and dinner is the Beijing on Salwa Road, near Ramada Junction.

Numerous options for international casual dining are clustered around Ramada Junction and the Khalifa Tennis & Squash Complex. Crepaway, on the western Salwa Road side of Ramada Junction, buzzes with life on Thursday evenings. Despite its name, it has a broad international menu of savoury dishes as well as desserts. Around Ramada Junction neon signs indicate myriad other options for casual dining. At the Khalifa Tennis & Squash complex, there's Fuddruckers and the Irish-American Bennigan's to choose from. While they're dry, alcohol is served at the nearby Amigo's Tex-Mex.

The most stylish café in Doha is Café Le Nôtre Paris at Ramada Junction, which has a good menu for main meals. Behind it, in the Al Emadi Center, Ma Maison de Thé offers a more regal Parisian ambience in its small tearoom. Across the parking lot, just beyond Starbucks, is the popular La Maison du Café.

Malls

Food courts in malls such as City Center Doha and the Landmark Shopping Mall offer the usual selection of Western fast-food outlets. At City Center these are joined by casual-dining restaurants such as Nando's, the South African chicken chain, and Applebee's. Of the various counter outlets, Tazaj is a regional chain that specialises in chicken meals. Its freshly baked Arabic bread is delicious. At Landmark, the Yum Yum Tree outlet does excellent pasta dishes. Locals head to the mall especially for its mixed red-and-white sauce, pasta-with-everything.

WHAT TO EAT

All menus account for the fact that the majority Muslim population can't eat or drink anything containing pork, alcohol or blood. Accordingly, all meat is halal (literally 'permissible'), which means the animal has been slaughtered according to Muslim law. Pork is not available at all in Qatar, but it is often substituted with beef 'bacon' and chicken sausages.

Common Arabian appetizers, heavily influenced by Lebanese cuisine, include hummus (the spelling varies), a dip made from chickpeas and *tahini* (sesame-seed paste) that's eaten with bread and goes especially well with carrot sticks or a side order of French fries; *moutabbal*, a paste of skinless grilled aubergine with *tahini* and lemon; *tabouleh*, a finely chopped parsley salad with mint, fresh tomatoes, onion and crushed wheat. topped with olive oil and lemon; and *fattoush*, an assorted green salad with toasted bread. Each of these would be included in a typical cold *mezze*.

Hot *mezze* includes the following appetisers: *kebeh*, fried minced lamb with crushed wheat, each of which is the shape and colour of a palm-sized American football; *sambousek*, samosa-style pastries filled with minced lamb and pine seeds or haloumi cheese or spinach; and *arayes*, bread stuffed with minced lamb, tomato and cheese.

Main courses tend to come from the grill. *Shawarma* is lamb or chicken sliced from a vertical spit and served with *toum*, a paste of crushed garlic and mayonnaise. Shish kebab comprises mutton chunks marinated with cumin and cinnamon and grilled on a skewer. *Shish tawouq* is similar, but with chicken pieces and served with a lemon-garlic sauce. A

Logaimat, made from egg, flour and saffron

Locally caught *hammour*, or red snapper

typical mixed grill would include mutton fillet, lamb chop, chicken kebab and *kofta* (lamb minced with parsley and onion). *Ghuzi* is a whole roast lamb served on a bed of rice with pine nuts.

Fish, such as locally caught *hammour* or red snapper, are typically grilled and served with sauces made from coriander, lemon and olive oil or tomato. North African couscous, granulated wheat flour, may accompany meat, chicken or fish dishes in some restaurants, but Arabian/Lebanese cuisine is generally eaten with pitta-style Arabic bread and a side plate of French fries, or rice.

Arabic desserts include *kashta*, which is clotted cream topped with pistachio, pine seeds and honey; *Umm Ali* (literally, 'Mother of Ali'), a bread-and-butter pudding with sultanas and coconut, topped with nuts; *esh asaraya* ('bread of the harem'), a cheesecake with cream topping; and *mehalabiya*, a milk custard made with pistachios and rose water.

For an on-the-move alternative to a sit-down meal, Arabic or Lebanese fast food comprises sandwiches made with Arabic bread and a variety of fillings, including *shawarma*, *shish tawouq* and falafel (mashed chickpeas and spices deep fried in flattened balls), served with a salad garnish. Also worth sampling is *manakeesh*, a round, pizza-like bread covered with *zatar*, a mixture of dried thyme, sesame seed, spices and olive oil.

WHAT TO DRINK

For obvious reasons there are no locally produced alcoholic drinks to savour. A comprehensive selection of international beers, wines and spirits is available in bars or restaurants linked to hotels and clubs.

Popular beverages throughout the Gulf are *shai* (tea) and *kahwa* (coffee). Traditional Arabian or Bedouin coffee is flavoured with cardamom and served in little cups without handles. Thick Turkish coffee is commonly served in restaurants. If you don't like it sweet, ask for medium-sweet *(wasat)* or without sugar *(bidoon sukkar)*. Tea, also served sweet, is commonly without milk and flavoured with cardamom or fresh mint. A fantastic selection of fresh juices – including guava, avocado and thick, creamy mixed fruit cocktails – is available in many restaurants and at specialist juice stalls.

Coffee is a popular beverage

To Help You Order…

Many of the service staff in restaurants are not native Arabic speakers, and you should have no problem getting by in English, particularly in hotels. Those that are Arabic-speakers – from the Levant or North Africa – will understand English, though for the sake of politeness here are a few Arabic phrases:

Do you have a table?	**Indaakum towla?**
Is there anyone here who speaks English?	**Haal yoojad ahad yatakaalam al-lugha al-ingleezia?**
May I see the menu, please?	**Laow samaht, ana ureed laeehat ataamm?**
Excuse me.	**Afwan.**
I don't eat meat	**La akul lahem.**
What do you recommend?	**Maatha tansah?**
I'd like…	**Ana ureed…**
May I have the bill, please?	**Fatoura, laow samaht.**

beef	**lahem bakar**	milk	**haleeb**
bread	**khobez**	pepper	**bahar**
chicken	**dajaj**	rice	**rouz**
coffee	**kahwa**	salad	**salata**
dessert	**helou**	salt	**melh**
fish	**samak**	sandwich	**sandweesh**
French fries	**batata makleea**	soup	**shorba**
		tea	**shai**
fruit	**fawakah**	vegetables	**khodra**
ice cream	**booza**	water	**mai**
lamb	**lahem harouf**		

…and Read a Menu

mezze	appetisers
jarjir	rocca leaves and onion
hummus	chickpea and *tahini* (sesame seed) paste

moutabbal	grilled aubergine, *tahini* and lemon paste
tabouleh	chopped parsley salad with mint, fresh tomatoes, onion and crushed wheat
fattoush	assorted green salad with toasted bread
salatat zatar	thyme salad with onions, lemon and olive oil
nakhi	boiled chickpeas
foul	fava-bean stew with garlic and lemon
bajella	local variation on boiled *foul*
kebeh	fried minced lamb with crushed wheat
sambousek	samosa-style pastries filled with minced lamb and pine seeds or haloumi cheese or spinach
arayes	bread stuffed with lamb, tomato and cheese
falafel	deep-fried mashed chickpeas and spices
roub	cucumber with yoghurt
couscous	granulated wheat flour
mashawee	grills
shawarma	grilled lamb or chicken sliced from a spit
toum	crushed garlic and mayonnaise paste
shish kebab	grilled mutton marinated with cumin and cinnamon
shish tawouq	grilled chicken pieces marinated with cumin and cinnamon
kofta	lamb minced with parsley and onion
ghuzi	whole roast lamb on rice with pine nuts
matchbous	spiced lamb with rice
hareis	slow-cooked wheat and lamb
hallaweeyat	desserts
kashta	clotted cream topped with pistachio, pine seeds and honey
Umm Ali	bread-and-butter pudding with sultanas and coconut and topped with nuts
esh asaraya	regional cheesecake with cream topping
mehalabiya	milk custard with pistachios and rose water
logaimat	fried balls made from egg, flour and saffron

Accommodation: If you're not on a package deal, the cost of a standard double room ranges from around QR350 ($96) per night in a two-star city-centre hotel to between QR930 ($255) and QR2,223 ($611) at a five-star resort hotel, depending on your choice. Add 17 percent tax and service charge to the basic room rate.

Meals and drinks: It's possible to eat for less than QR55 ($15) per person in no-nonsense street restaurants serving Lebanese and Indian food. A filling *shawarma* sandwich is around QR5 ($1.4). *Dosa* and *idly* are similarly priced. A meal in a Western-style casual-dining restaurant costs around QR65 ($18) per person without drinks. For fine-dining restaurants, budget for upwards of QR150 ($41) per person without drinks.

Cans of soft drinks start at QR1 ($0.30) in shops, but are marked up in restaurants. Freshly made juices cost between QR5 ($1.40) and QR10 ($2.70). A tall caffè latte at Starbucks costs QR12 ($3.30). Imported alcoholic drinks are generally more expensive than they would be in the West.

Local transport: Most taxi fares around Doha will be around QR10 ($2.70). The metering in the cleaner, more comfortable Karwa taxis starts at QR3 ($0.80) and runs at QR1 ($0.30) per kilometre. The fare from the airport to any destination in Doha shouldn't be more than QR25 ($7).

An organised trip with a tour company to Khor Al Udaid (the Inland Sea) costs around QR200 ($55) for a half-day and QR300 ($82.4) for a full day.

BUSINESS HOURS

The local weekend is Fri–Sat. Government ministries and departments are open Sun–Thur 7am–2pm. Commercial offices tend to operate Sun–Thur 7.30am–noon and 3.30–7.30pm.

Shop opening hours are generally Sat–Thur 8.30am–12.30pm and 4–8pm, and Fri 4–8pm, but outlets in malls tend to remain open Sat–Thur 10am–10pm and Fri 3–10pm.

C

CAMPING

Camping is a popular weekend activity among Doha residents, in particular, with Khor Al Udaid (the Inland Sea) and Zikreet among the favoured destinations. While there's ample room to pitch a tent in Qatar's desert landscape, there's a distinct lack of organised campsites with facilities provided, so you'll have to carry along everything you'll need, from water to gas.

The desert is one of the harshest environments known to man. The reality is that to camp anywhere worthwhile in Qatar, you'll need a four-wheel-drive vehicle to get there and you should never attempt to drive off-road unless you've done it before and are accompanied by at least one other vehicle driven by an experienced driver.

All things considered, by far the most sensible option for visitors wanting to camp in Qatar is to book an overnight trip with a tour company that will take care of all the arrangements, from tents to belly-dancer. While that might satisfy the desire to sleep outdoors, it comes at a price, so there won't be much of a cost saving to enjoy.

CAR HIRE (see also DRIVING)

With a lack of public transport to attractions outside Doha, hiring a car is one of the best ways of exploring the country. In fact, unless you're fortunate enough to have a local host, it's the only alternative to taking organised tours.

Qatar is well served by a number of international and local car-hire companies:

Avis tel: 462 2180
Hertz tel: 462 2563
Budget tel: 462 2678
Thrifty tel: 462 1180
National tel: 487 8068

Most of these have kiosks in the arrivals area of Doha Airport. The typical daily rate for a mid-size saloon is around QR150 ($41), including insurance and unlimited mileage.

Most national driving licences are recognised, but it's a good idea to have a valid International Driving Licence with you as back-up. Without a Qatari licence, cars can only be hired within seven days of arrival. If you've been in Qatar for longer than seven days, you'll need to obtain a temporary (six-month) Qatari driving permit from the Driving Licence Section of the Traffic Department (tel: 489 0666). The cost is QR150 ($41). Those with an International Driving Licence can drive for up to six months after their arrival in Qatar, but only in private cars, not rental vehicles.

Car-hire companies require a credit-card guarantee, though you can settle in cash when you return the vehicle.

I want to hire a car…	**Ureed astajer siyara…**
now/tomorrow	**towa/bukra**
day/week	**yom/isboa**
International Driving Licence	**tasreah kiyadah dowli**
local driving permit	**rukhsat kiyadah**

CLIMATE AND WHEN TO GO

Qatar is an arid, desert nation with mild, pleasant winters and very hot, humid summers. While the PR spin on the country's climate is that it 'enjoys sunshine just about every day of the year', the reality is that you can't be out in the sun for long periods at any time of year. Summertime is when people spend more time indoors – kept cool by air conditioning.

The period June–Sept (hotels' low season) is particularly hot, with temperatures topping 45°C (115°F) during the day and falling to a minimum of 18°C (64°F) at night, with up to 90 percent humidity. However, from November to April the weather is glorious, with monthly peaks between 28°C (82°F) and 38°C (100°F) during the day and falling as low as 7°C (44°F) at night. Humidity also falls considerably. Weather-wise, this is undoubtedly the best time to visit, but commensurate with the fall in temperatures is a rise in accommodation costs. What rain there is – the annual average is just 70 mm (2¾ ins) – tends to fall on isolated days between October and March, when heavy morning fog can also occur.

CLOTHING (see also CLIMATE)

There are cultural and practical considerations to what you should and shouldn't pack for a visit to Qatar. The country is conservative by Western standards, and visitors – men and women – are expected to dress modestly. While swimming trunks and bikinis are fine at the beach, it's not acceptable to expose the body in other public areas, such as residential neighbourhoods near beaches, or in *souqs* and malls. Revealing too much skin will cause offence – and that goes as much for men baring their torsos as it does for women revealing too much of theirs. It's fine to expose arms and legs, but shoulders should be covered and shorts or skirts shouldn't ride too high. It's particularly important to dress modestly during the Muslim holy month of Ramadan.

Practically, consider that Qatar is hot in summer and warm in winter, so lightweight cottons and linens are advisable. Winter evenings can be surprisingly cool, so it will be necessary to pack a cardigan or jumper, particularly if you want to enjoy an alfresco evening meal or if you're planning to attend an open-air event at night. There's also a chance of rain in winter, so light rainwear could come in handy.

CRIME AND SAFETY

Crime is rare in Qatar. Generally, visitors won't encounter criminal activity and needn't be concerned about being extra cautious with their possessions. Most people feel safe on the streets of Doha even late at night. Certainly, there are no neighbourhoods to avoid or gangs of rabble-rousing youths to steer clear of. That said, it would be wise to maintain the usual precautions you're in the habit of keeping elsewhere in the world, and visitors should obtain comprehensive travel and medical insurance before travelling.

The US-led 'war on terror' has led to concerns for the safety of citizens of countries associated with American military activity in the region. Qatar is no exception, and vigilance against terrorism is recommended. However, the one incident against Western civilians in Qatar – a car-bomb attack on the Doha Players' Theatre in March 2005 – seems to have been an isolated attack, carried out by an Egyptian. Qatar remains an extremely safe country, and the Qataris themselves are very hospitable towards outsiders.

I have lost my passport…	**Reyaht al jawaz…**
wallet	**disdan**
handbag	**shuntah**

CUSTOMS AND ENTRY FORMALITIES

Visas are available on arrival at Doha Airport for business and leisure travellers from 33 countries, including the United States, UK, Ireland, Canada, Australia, New Zealand, most of Europe and selected Asian nations. The cost is QR55 ($15). The passport-control officers who issue the visas refuse to accept cash payment, even in Qatari Riyals, and will require a credit or debit card. If you don't have plastic you may be directed to a nearby counter that issues prepaid cards, but those available may be of a high value that you're unlikely to redeem during a short visit. The visas issued are for 21 days.

Hotels and airlines can assist visitors of other nationalities to secure 14-day visas.

Passport-holders from more than 30 countries can also apply for Qatari visas online ('e-visas') at <www.e.gov.qa>. The countries include the United States, UK, Ireland, Canada, Australia, New

Zealand, Austria, Belgium, France, Germany, Iceland, Italy, Luxembourg, Monaco, the Netherlands, Portugal, Spain, Switzerland, Vatican City, Sweden, Norway, Finland, Denmark, Greece, Singapore, Malaysia, Hong Kong, South Korea, Japan and SAR. However, there's little benefit in getting an e-visa if you qualify for one on arrival.

Visas issued for 21 days can be renewed once for a further seven days; 14-day visas can be renewed once for a further 14 days. The cost for both renewals is QR50 ($14). The renewal office is at Doha Airport (tel: 465 6615; open Sun–Thur 6am–1pm). Further information about visas can be found at the Qatar Ministry of Interior website <www.moi.gov.qa>.

It's illegal to bring alcohol, including duty-free purchases, non-prescription drugs, guns and ammunition into Qatar. Non-Muslim religious material, such as Bibles, are allowed in for personal use, but not for proselytising.

(I have) nothing forbidden	**mafeesh mamnu'at**

D

DRIVING (see also CAR HIRE)

Qataris drive on the right side of the road. Vehicles are, therefore, left-hand drive. Qatar's road system is mostly adequate, but drivers should beware of unexpected potholes on back roads and even on some highways outside Doha. Outside the capital there's also a possibility that camels will wander across the path of an oncoming vehicle, so be cautious on desert roads, particularly at night on sections that aren't well lit. Lane discipline is not great, so on roads with more than a single lane in one direction, be aware of what's happening behind and on either side of you before manoeuvring. Also, taxi drivers may swerve or stop suddenly if they spot a fare at the roadside, so keep a safe distance behind them.

The wearing of seat belts is compulsory for drivers and front-seat passengers. The fine for not complying is QR100 ($27). Speed limits are set at 50, 60, 80, 100 and 120kph. Many roads are under radar surveillance. The penalty for speeding is a fine of between QR300 and QR500 ($82–137). The penalty for jumping a red light is a QR1,000 ($275) fine. The fine for parking in unauthorised areas varies from QR300 to QR1,000 ($82–275).

If you're involved in a road accident, stop where you are and wait for the police, even if you're blocking traffic. Although it may seem the right thing to do in the case of minor shunts, don't pull over to the side of the road. A police report on every level of accident is required for insurance claims. If you're stopped by the police at any time, you must be able to produce your driving licence and car-hire/insurance papers (originals, not copies) there and then. If you don't have them on you, expect an on-the-spot fine of QR200 ($55).

Unless you're an experienced off-road driver, you shouldn't consider renting a four-wheel-drive to head to desert destinations outside Doha. The desert is one of the harshest environments known to man and there's a particular technique to driving in it.

E

ELECTRICITY

The mains electricity in Qatar is 220–240v + 6 percent with a frequency of 50 Hertz.

EMBASSIES AND CONSULATES

Visitors from Australia, Canada, Ireland and New Zealand should note that their countries don't have embassies in Qatar, but are represented by those located in neighbouring Gulf states.

Australia Level 14, Al Muhairy Centre, Abu Dhabi, United Arab Emirates; tel: +971 2 634 6100; <abudhabi.embassy@dfat.gov.au>.

Canada Daiyah, 24 Al-Mutawakkel Street, Area 4, Kuwait; tel: +965 256 3025; <www.dfait-maeci.gc.ca/kuwait>.
Ireland Diplomatic Quarter, Riyadh, Kingdom of Saudi Arabia; tel: +966 1 488 2300; <irishembassy@awalnet.net.sa>.
New Zealand Diplomatic Quarter, Riyadh, Kingdom of Saudi Arabia; tel: +966 1 488 7988; <nzembassy@awalnet.net.sa>.
South Africa Stand 801, Saha 570, Plot 5, West Bay Lagoon, Doha; tel: 485 7111; <saembdoha@qatar.net.qa>.
United Kingdom Opposite Qatar Bowling Centre, Rumeila, Doha; tel: 442 1991; <www.britishembassy.gov.uk>.
United States D Ring Road/22 February Street; tel: 488 4101; <www.qatar.usembassy.gov>.

EMERGENCIES

Dial 999 for police, fire or ambulance.

G

GETTING THERE

The point of arrival for most visitors to Qatar is Doha International Airport, though cruise ships do dock occasionally at Doha Port. There's a land border crossing from Saudi Arabia at Abu Samra, on the southwest of the peninsula, which is commonly used by GCC nationals, but few other international visitors.

A planned 40-km (25-mile) Friendship Causeway that will link Qatar and the island state of Bahrain is unlikely to open before 2010, and another causeway linking Qatar to the emirate of Abu Dhabi in the United Arab Emirates (UAE) has been announced, but with no timetable for construction. For now, visitors planning to travel between Qatar and the UAE should fly, as the land border between the two countries that appears on many maps no longer exists.

Doha Airport, the international hub for Qatar Airways, is served by regular scheduled flights from Europe. British Airways has a daily flight from London Heathrow. Air France and KLM are among other European carriers flying to Doha. The flying time from London to Doha is around seven hours. Currently, there are no direct flights from the United States or Canada. North American visitors, therefore, must consider transiting through a European hub. Travellers from Australia and New Zealand might consider flying Emirates to Dubai. The onward flight from Dubai to Doha is just 40 minutes. Qatar Airways and its partner airlines also link into Australia and New Zealand from the Asian hub cities.

GUIDES AND TOURS

While most sites in Qatar are accessible to independent travellers, prior permission is required for entry to certain others (eg, the Weaponry Museum and the Al Maha Sanctuary oryx reserve at Al Shahaniya), and outside Doha directional signage for heritage and tourist attractions is lacking (the rock carvings at Jebel Jassasiya are especially hard to find).

In addition, Qatar's major natural attraction, the Inland Sea (Khor Al Udaid), is challenging to reach because of the wildness of the desert terrain: you can only get there in a four-wheel-drive vehicle and you need to be an experienced off-road driver to try. For these reasons, it's recommended that you forgo at least one or two days of independent exploration to take an organised tour.

Qatar's leading tour companies are Qatar International Tours (QIT; tel: 466 7782; <www.qit-qatar.com/tours>), Gulf Adventures (tel: 431 5555; <www.gulf-adventures.com>) and Arabian Adventures (tel: 436 1461).

For solo travellers or couples, the one obstacle to booking a desert trip with a tour company is that you'll be expected to pay for a minimum of three seats. The best way around this is to round up fellow-travellers to make up the difference, or get your name on a waiting list a few days before you plan to go, in the hope that others will do the same.

H

HEALTH AND MEDICAL CARE

Medical and dental treatment is available to visitors at government hospitals and regional health centres. The main government hospital in Doha is Hamad General Hospital (tel: 439 4444). Charges are high and health insurance is essential.

Visitors should take precautions to avoid illness brought about by the intense sun and heat. Those out in the sun even for short periods of time should cover their heads: even when there's cloud cover or a breeze, the scalp can burn. A high-factor sun block should be applied to exposed skin, not forgetting the ears, the back of the neck and the tops of sandaled feet. Drink plenty of water to avoid dehydration.

Get a doctor…	**Jeeb doktor…**
quickly	**bisoorah**
hospital	**mustashfa**

HOLIDAYS

Qatar's fixed annual holidays are Accession Day on 27 June and Independence Day on 3 September. Other holidays – such as Eid Al Fitr and Eid Al Adha – are linked to the holy month of Ramadan, which moves forward by 11 days each year, according to the Islamic calendar.

L

LANGUAGE

Arabic is the official language in Qatar, but English is widely spoken. It's unlikely that you'll encounter any difficulty using English in hotels, restaurants and shopping malls, as many of the staff aren't Arabic speakers themselves. That said, wherever you meet someone you know is an Arabic-speaker, it would be polite to have a few words and phrases committed to memory.

hello	**marhaba**
welcome	**ahlan wa-sahlan (ahlan)**
peace be with you (greeting)	**as-salaam alaykum**
and with you be peace (response)	**wa-alaykum as-salaam**
excuse me	**afwan**
good morning (greeting)	**sabah al khayr**
good morning (response)	**sabah al nour**
good evening (greeting)	**masaa al khayr**
good evening (response)	**masaa al nour**
my name is…	**ana ismi…**
what is your name?	**shou ismac?**
how are you?	**kayf haalak?**
well	**zein**
you're welcome	**afwan**
please	**min fadlak**
thank you	**shukran**
yes	**naam**
no	**la**
goodbye, peace be with you	**maa as-salaama**

M

MAPS

GeoProjects <www.geoprojects-maps.co.uk> produces a regularly updated 1:230,000 scale map of Qatar and central Doha in its Arab World Map Library series. The map is available internationally, but can be hard to get hold of in Qatar itself. The best map of central Doha, showing hotels, attractions, shopping malls and embassies, is reproduced in the locally-published information guide, *Marhaba* <marhaba@qatar.net.qa>. If you're hiring a car, don't rely on hire companies to provide you with a good map – come with your own.

MEDIA

The two daily English-language newspapers in Qatar are *Gulf Times* and *The Peninsula*. Both have the latest local and international news, business and sport. The three Arabic dailies – *Al-Sharq*, *Arrayah* and *Al-Watan* – are not available in English translation. The main English-language guides to what's on are tailored to expatriate residents rather than visitors, but are very useful nonetheless: one is *Marhaba*, published three times a year and containing extensive listings for eating out, shopping and sports, as well as lengthy sections on health, education, banking, motoring and oil and gas; the other is the slimmer *Qatar Happening*, which appears monthly.

Satellite and cable TV, with international news channels such as CNN, BBC World and Sky News, are widely available in hotels. Al Jazeera, the Qatar-based satellite channel, is in Arabic, but there are plans for an English equivalent. Qatar Television (QTV) offers Channel 1 and Channel 2, the latter containing mainly English programming. Qatar Radio's English service is on 97.5FM, except between 1.15 and 4pm, when French is broadcast.

Have you any English papers?	**Hal fee jereeda ingliziya?**

MONEY MATTERS

The currency in Qatar is the Qatari riyal (QR), which is pegged to the US dollar at the rate of QR3.64 to $1. There are 100 dirhams in a riyal. The notes in circulation are QR1, 5, 10, 100 and 500. The most common coins are 25 dirhams and 50 dirhams.

Banks are open Sun–Thur 7.30am–1pm, but the best places to change foreign currency and traveller's cheques into riyals are the numerous currency exchanges that work a seven-day week, opening Sat–Thur 8am–noon and 4–8 pm, Fri 4–8 pm. Among them are Almana Exchange (tel: 442 4226), Alfardan Exchange & Finance (tel: 440 8214), National Exchange (tel: 432 3359), City Exchange (tel: 443 5060), Gulf Finance & Exchange (tel: 442 8211) and Habib Qatar International Finance (tel: 432 8853).

Traveller's cheques are widely accepted. Major international credit and debit cards are accepted in large shops, restaurants and hotels.

There are no restrictions on the import or export of either local or foreign currency. Israeli currency, however, is prohibited.

I want to change dollars	**Ureed usareef dollar**

P

PHOTOGRAPHY

Ask permission before taking a photograph of anyone. If language is a barrier, pointing to your camera should be enough to get a yes or no response. Qatari women generally don't like having their picture taken, even when covered, and simply resting a camera on a restaurant table may result in complaints to management if it happens to be pointing their way. Don't take photographs of military bases.

I want a camera film/battery	**Ureed film kamara/battariya**

POLICE

The police have a visible presence in Qatar: their blue-and-white vehicles are often parked at busy roundabouts during rush hour. The emergency number for the police is 999.

POST OFFICES

Doha's General Post Office (open: Sunday–Thursday 7am–8pm; Saturday 8–11am, 5–8pm; closed Friday) is located in West Bay, just back from the Corniche. There are also suburban and regional post offices, including one at Doha Airport which is open 24 hours a day.

The cost of sending a postcard to most Western countries is around 200 dirhams. Airmail to Europe or North America takes up to one week to arrive. International courier companies operating in Qatar include DHL (tel: 462 1202), FedEx (tel: 466 1722) and UPS (tel: 432 2444).

a stamp for England, please	**tab'a bareed Ingilterra, min fadlak**
airmail	**bareed jowi**

PUBLIC TRANSPORT

For 'public transport' read 'taxis', because the bus service in Qatar is infrequent and trains non-existent. Doha is a relatively compact city, so most taxi fares will be around QR10 ($2.7). At present there are two options for taxis: the ubiquitous orange-and-white cars tend to be older and less comfortable than the recently introduced turquoise Karwa taxis (tel: 458 8888). There's no central despatch for the former, which are to be gradually phased out. While it is possible to book a Karwa cab, you may have to wait a while for it to arrive. At city-centre locations, therefore, it's best to hail a cab in the street.

However, for travels from places where taxis aren't such a common sight (eg, Doha Golf Club) consider booking a slightly more costly limousine from Al Afdhal (tel: 488 0177) or Fox Transport (tel: 462 2777). Most hotels operate airport pick-ups and drop-offs, either by limousine or shuttle bus.

R

RELIGION

Islam is the official religion in Qatar, but there is freedom of worship for Christians on the understanding that they don't proselytise. Contact details for Christian churches in Doha are published in the *Marhaba* information guide. Bibles for personal use can be carried into the country.

S

SMOKING

Qatar has introduced tobacco-control laws banning smoking in public places, such as restaurants, shopping centres, sports venues and on public transport. The fine if you're caught breaking the ban is QR100 ($27).

T

TELEPHONE

The international dialling code for Qatar is 00 974. Qatar Telecom (Qtel; tel: 440 0400) provides international direct dialling (IDD) to 215 countries. The code for dialling internationally from Qatar is a single 0, not 00.

Well-maintained Qtel payphones are prominently located in public areas and can be found in malls, usually near the prayer room or toilet area. A local call on a public phone costs 50 fils (half a dirham) for three minutes. It's also possible to call internationally on such phones. Prepaid phone cards are available from Qtel, bookstores and supermarkets. The number for directory enquiries is 180, where assistance is provided in English as well as Arabic.

Roaming mobile-phone users will gain access to the Qatarnet GSM 900 network.

TIME DIFFERENCES

Qatar is GMT plus three hours, throughout the year.

TIPPING

Tipping is appreciated, but is not expected. Unusually, taxi drivers do not expect a tip. A service charge is often added to bills in hotels and most restaurants, otherwise a 10 per cent tip would be appropriate.

TOILETS

Western-style toilets are commonly found in hotels and restaurants.

toilet	**al hammam**

TOURIST INFORMATION (see also WEBSITES)

The Qatar Tourism Authority (QTA) (tel: 441 1555; <www.qatartourism.gov.qa>) is the government's tourism promotion agency. In addition, Qatar embassies should be willing to help with enquiries. Qatar's embassy in Washington DC has a particularly informative website: <www.qatarembassy.net>. Generally, there's a lack of tourism information in Qatar itself. Published guides aside, hotel staff are the primary source of information on where to go and what to do.

TRAVELLERS WITH DISABILITIES

Travellers with disabilities aren't especially well provided for in Qatar. In addition to stairs, many modern hotels have ramps allowing for wheelchair access, as well as elevators inside, of course. In larger shopping malls there's usually an elevator alternative to an escalator, and enlarged cubicles in public toilets. But the facilities in most of Qatar's historic and cultural attractions don't cater for people with disabilities.

(referred to locally as the 'eastern side'), the hotel is less than 10 minutes' drive from the airport and old city centre, and 15 minutes by car from West Bay. It has its own marina and private beach, floodlit tennis courts, pool and spa. Restaurants include Salsa Tex-Mex, Asia Live! and the Indian Taj Rasoi, which make for a lively atmosphere off the lobby in the evenings. 350 rooms in two separate buildings.

Mövenpick $$$ *Al Corniche Street, tel: 429 1111, fax: 429 1100, <www.movenpickdoha.com>.* The four-star Mövenpick, which opened in 2001, is separated from the Corniche by a small park. A short walk from Qatar National Museum, it's around 10 minutes' drive from the airport and a short cab-ride to the New Souqs area and city-centre attractions such as the Wind-Tower House and Al Koot Fort. The six-storey hotel has 154 extra-large, comfortable rooms with fine views over Doha Port and the bay. It has a small outdoor pool, a spa, a gymnasium on the ground level, and wireless internet connection in the lobby and other common areas. The hotel's Piano Piano jazz lounge is a popular venue in the evenings.

Oasis Hotel & Beach Club $$ *Ras Abu Abboud Street, tel: 442 4424, fax: 432 7096, email: <oasis@oasishotel-doha.com>, <www.oasishotel-doha.com>.* Located between the Marriott and the Doha Club, less than 10 minutes' drive from the airport, the four-star Oasis is the best value waterfront hotel in Doha. Offering a panoramic view of Doha Bay, it has a private beach and two pools. Other facilities include tennis and squash courts, a gym and children's playground. Its restaurants include the à la carte Al-Nakheel as well as Italian and Chinese options. 160 rooms.

DOHA CITY CENTRE

Al Bustan $$ *Al Muthaf Street, tel: 432 8888, fax: 443 6111, email: <albustan@qatar.net.qa>, <www.qatar.net.qa/albustan>.* Just off the Corniche, a short walk along Al Muthaf Street from Museum/Perfume Roundabout and a stone's throw from Qatar

National Museum, the three-star Al Bustan is a friendly street-front boutique hotel that's best-known for its *shisha* (water pipe) tent, the best in Qatar, which bustles with life between 6.30–11pm daily. Doha Airport is less than 10 minutes' drive away. The Corniche is a short walk left out of the front door, the New Souqs area a longer walk right along Al Muthaf/Ali Bin Abdullah Street.

Al Sadd Merweb Hotel $$ *Al Sadd Street, tel: 447 1111, fax: 447 1117, <www.merweb-hotel.com>*. Just west of C Ring Road/ Suhaim Bin Hamad Street, 'the Merweb' is neither very close to the city centre sights nor West Bay, but it does have the advantage of being just one roundabout away from the myriad eateries and trendy hang-outs at Ramada Junction. A medium-sized three-star hotel, the Merweb's rooms are clean and comfortable, but a gym is all there is in the way of recreational facilities. Doha's nightlife is said to start at the hotel's mezzanine-level Cloudnyn discothèque.

Gulf Horizon $$ *Al Jabr Street, near Souq Al Jabor, New Markets area, tel: 443 2525, fax: 441 0435, email: <ghorizon@ qatar.net.qa>*. This three-star city-centre hotel is about as close as you can stay to Doha's *souqs*. Located in a backstreet near the modern-build Souq Al Jabor, Gulf Horizon Hotel is within 10 minutes' walk of no less than eight *souqs*, including the most traditional of them all, Souq Waqif. Also within walking distance are the Corniche's Water Pots Roundabout and the Museum of Islamic Arts.

Mercure Grand $$$ *Wadi Musheireb Street, tel: 446 2222, fax: 443 9186, email: <mercuredoha@qatar.net.qa>, <www.mercure doha.com>*. Formerly the Sofitel, this four-star street-front hotel, built in 1982, is a short walk along Wadi Musheireb Street from Dhow Roundabout near Al Koot Fort, and around 15 minutes' drive from Doha Airport. It has an outdoor pool, fitness centre and sauna, and restaurants offering Mediterranean and English cuisine. Its 174 rooms have recently been refurbished to very high standards.

New Capital Hotel $ *Wadi Musheireb Street, tel: 444 5445, fax: 444 2233.* Situated just along the street from the Mercure, the smaller, 84-room New Capital Hotel is a conveniently located, lower price alternative to more upmarket city-centre accommodation. A three-star hotel, it has no sports or recreational facilities.

Qatar Palace Hotel $ *44 Al Asmakh Street, tel: 442 1515, fax: 432 1515, email: <qatarpal@qatar.net.qa>, <www.qatarpal.com.qa>.* The three-star, 45-room Qatar Palace Hotel is another no-frills alternative for budget-conscious travellers. What it lacks in sports and recreational facilities is compensated by its proximity to Souq Al Najada, the Wind-Tower House, Al Koot Fort and Souq Waqif. As with all city-centre hotels, the airport is just 15 minutes' drive away.

Ramada Hotel Doha $$$$ *Salwa Road, near Ramada Junction, tel: 441 7417, fax: 441 0941, email: <ramada@qatar.net.qa>, <www.ramada-doha.com>.* Built in 1980, the four-star Ramada is located at what locals consider to be the centre of Doha, the junction of C Ring Road and Salwa Road, otherwise known as Ramada Junction, after the venerable hotel. While casual-dining restaurants and cafés abound in the streets around, the hotel itself is a centre for nightlife, with several restaurants that are popular with local and expat residents as well as guests, and a lively bar, Shehrazad Lounge Bar and Irish Terrace. Sports and recreational facilities include an outdoor pool, tennis courts and fully equipped fitness centre. 320 rooms.

Regency $$ *10 Al Asmakh Street, tel: 436 3363, fax: 432 5232, email: <hregency@qatar.net.qa>, <www.hotel-regency.com>.* Like the Qatar Palace Hotel, The Regency is on Al Asmakh Street, a short walk from Souq Al Najada, the Wind-Tower House, Al Koot Fort and Souq Waqif. A typical room includes satellite TV, international direct dialling (IDD) telephone and voice mail, minibar and en suite bathroom. The hotel has no sports or recreational facilities.

Rydges Plaza $$ *Abu Firas Street, Al Bidda, tel: 438 5444, fax: 438 5445, email: <reservations_doha@rydges.com>, <www.rydges.com>*. Part of the Australian-owned Rydges group, the four-star Rydges Plaza, which opened in 2003, is centrally located in a modern tower between the old city centre and West Bay, two streets behind the Corniche. The lobby boasts an impressively high atrium and a popular Italian restaurant, Il Rustico. Glass elevators carry guests to the hotel's 136 rooms, rooftop outdoor pool, health club and one of Doha's most popular nightspots, Aussie Legends sports bar and grill.

Shezan Hotel $ *Ahmed Bin Ali Street, between the Athletes' Village and City Center mall, tel: 486 5225, fax: 486 5267, email: <shezanhtl@qatar.net.qa>, <www.freewebz.com/shezanhotel>*. A two-star offering with 60 rooms and one suite, the Shezan is one of the relatively few low-cost alternatives to Doha's growing number of premium hotels. It's a 15- to 20-minute drive from the airport, less than 10 minutes' cab-ride from the Corniche four roundabouts away, and a short walk from the Athletes' Village constructed for the 2006 Doha Asian Games. The hotel has a Pakistani restaurant.

WEST BAY

Four Seasons $$$$$ *West Bay Complex, tel: 494 8888, fax: 494 8282, <www.fourseasons.com/doha>*. An 18-storey neoclassical building influenced by Spain's Alhambra Palace and capped by two arabesque crowns, the landmark Four Seasons is 12km (7.5 miles) or 15 minutes' drive from Doha Airport. Opened in 2005, this five-star jewel in the West Bay Complex, near the Sheraton Hotel at the northern end of the Corniche, has 232 luxuriously appointed guest rooms, including 57 suites. Conveniently located for Qatar International Exhibition Centre and within walking distance of City Center mall, the hotel has several top eateries, including the Italian Il Teatro, a private beach and pool, a 110-berth marina, two outdoor tennis courts, a fitness centre and spa. Arguably the best hotel in Doha.

InterContinental Doha $$$$ *off Aladdin Roundabout, tel: 484 4444, fax: 483 9555, email: <doha@interconti.com>, <www.intercontinental.com>.* When the 245-room InterContinental opened in time for Qatar's hosting of the Organisation of Islamic Congress (OIC) Summit in 2000, it was the first five-star hotel to be built in Qatar for 18 years and the forerunner in a rush of five-star openings and announcements in the first years of the 21st century. Located a little way out of the city, 20 minutes' drive from the airport, but just five minutes' drive from Doha Golf Club, the InterCon has a splendid 400-m private beach, the largest outdoor pool of any Qatar hotel, an upscale health club and a range of facilities for water sports, tennis and squash. Popular restaurants in the hotel include Sultan Ibrahim for seafood, Za Moda for contemporary Italian cuisine, and Paloma Tex-Mex, which has dancing from midnight to 2am daily. Its Amwaj restaurant is a popular venue for Friday brunch.

The Ritz-Carlton Doha $$$$ *West Bay Lagoon, tel: 484 8000, fax: 484 8484, email: <info.doha@ritzcarlton.com>, <www.ritzcarlton.com>.* Located some distance from the old city centre and the commercial heart of West Bay, but closer than any other hotel to Doha Golf Club, the 374-room, five-star Ritz-Carlton opened in 2001 for Qatar's hosting of the 4th Ministerial Conference of the World Trade Organisation (WTO). Its facilities include indoor and outdoor pools, indoor tennis and squash courts, a fitness centre, spa and 235-slip marina, though curiously for a coastal hotel, it does not have a beach. Restaurants include the French fine-dining La Mer, which offers a panoramic view of the Arabian Gulf from the 23rd floor, the Italian Porcini and The Lagoon, a popular venue for Friday brunches. The hotel's Lobby Lounge is a stylish venue for afternoon tea.

Sheraton Doha Hotel and Resort $$$$$ *Al Corniche Street, tel: 485 4444, fax: 483 2323, email: <sheraton.doha@sheraton.com>, <www.sheraton.com/doha>.* You'll be joining a long list of distinguished guests if you stay at the landmark pyramid-shaped Sheraton: US President George Bush, Egyptian President

Hosni Mubarrak, the late Diana, Princess of Wales, Mohammed Ali and Bjorn Borg have all stayed here. The iconic 16-storey hotel, a symbol of modern Qatar and still considered by many as one of the best hotels in the Middle East, was built in 1982 and renovated at a cost of $20 million for its 20th anniversary in 2002. Each of its 363 rooms has its own balcony with views of the Arabian Gulf. Recreational facilities include a private beach and lagoon with sailing academy, swimming pools, tennis and squash courts and gym. The hotel's top-floor Al Shaheen fine-dining restaurant offers the best panoramic view of Doha Bay and the Corniche, which begins virtually at the foot of the hotel. Qatar International Exhibition Centre and City Center mall are within walking distance.

OUTSIDE DOHA

MESAIEED

Sealine Beach Resort $$ *Mesaieed, on the road to Khor Al Udaid (Inland Sea), tel: 477 2722, fax: 477 2733, email: <sbr@ qatar.net.qa>, <www.qnhc.com>*. Located 60km (37 miles) or 40 minutes' drive south of Doha, the four-star Sealine Beach Resort, built in 1994, is a popular weekend retreat for residents of Doha. The nearest hotel to Khor Al Udaid (the Inland Sea), which is a further 55km (35 miles) south through the sand dunes, and, for the moment at least, the only beach resort outside the capital, Sealine offers 35 rooms and two suites in the main hotel building and 20 three-bedroom villas and 20 studio-style chalets – all are sea-facing. Facilities include an Olympic-size swimming pool, a lagoon-style pool, outdoor tennis courts and gym. The resort's water-sports centre offers jet-skis for hire, while forays into the surrounding dunes can be enjoyed on quad bike, camel or pony. Its Pearl Restaurant offers an à la carte menu of international and oriental cuisines. The resort also has a poolside snack bar and Dunes Bar.

Recommended Restaurants

Qatar's best restaurants are concentrated in the capital, many of them in the city's five-star hotels and clubs, where alcohol is served. To ensure the best possible table – indeed, any table on busy Thursday evenings – you should call to make a reservation in advance.

Hotels and clubs aside, there are a number of notable eateries on the streets of Doha, particularly around Ramada Junction/Salwa Road and the Khalifa Tennis & Squash Complex. An evening stroll through either location will provide you with several options for good food. Family- and casual-dining restaurants abound. Those are not considered here, though several options are mentioned in passing in the Where to Go section.

To keep abreast of the latest restaurant openings and promotional offers, scan the editorial and adverts in Qatar's *Marhaba* information guide and the monthly events guide *Qatar Happening.*

The price categories below, in US dollars, are based on a three-course meal per person excluding drinks, though in reality two generous courses may be filling enough, and in a street environment you might consider moving on to a nearby café for dessert and coffee.

$$$$	over $40
$$$	$30–40
$$	$20–30
$	under $20

DOHA CITY CENTRE

Al Layali $$ *Souq Najd, Salwa Road, tel: 431 0005.* Probably the best Lebanse restaurant in town. Fresh herbs specially brought in from Lebanon accentuate a delicious array of lamb, chicken and fresh fish entrées in an evocative Middle Eastern atmosphere. Also known for its top quality *shisha.* Open daily noon–midnight.

Aussie Legends $$ *Rydges Plaza Hotel, Abu Firas Street, Al Bidda, tel: 438 5444.* A lively sports bar that's primarily a drinking venue, but also offers excellent grills, including the best burger in town. Open Sat–Thur 4pm–3am, Fri noon–3am.

The Beijing $ *Salwa Road, tel: 435 8688.* A popular Chinese restaurant, probably the city's best, vying for your custom in an area abounding with far less satisfying fast food and casual-dining alternatives. Open for lunch and dinner daily 11.30am–3.30pm and 5.30–11.30pm.

Café Batteel $ *Salwa Road, tel: 444 1414.* A friendly local eatery that offers fine dining as well as coffee, pastries and Arabic sweets. Open daily 8am–midnight.

Café Le Nôtre Paris $–$$ *Salwa Road, near Ramada Junction.* Doha's in-crowd – local men and women in national dress and Armani- and Prada-clad Arab expatriates – gather for delicious appetizers, mains and desserts in a hip indoor setting or, during cooler months, on the black-tile terrace overlooking Salwa Road. Open Sat–Thur 8am–11.30pm, Fri 8–11am and 12.30–11.30pm.

Chingari $$–$$ *Ramada Hotel, Salwa Road, near Ramada Junction, tel: 441 7417.* An Indian restaurant in a hotel setting near Ramada Junction, which means you can have a tipple with your tandoori. Open for dinner daily 7–10.30pm.

Crepaway $–$$ *Al Mouthanna Complex, Salwa Road, near Ramada Junction, tel: 465 5830.* A funky casual-dining outlet with a broad international menu – both sweet and savoury – that's particularly popular with youthful Lebanese expatriates who know the chain from Beirut. Open Sat–Wed 6.30am–12.30am, Thur–Fri 6.30am–1.30am.

The Garden $ *Al Kharaba Street.* Award-winning, excellent-value-for-money, no-nonsense south Indian restaurant in a downtown area known for its textile shops. Serves up *dosa* and *idly* for breakfast from 7 to 11am every day and is open for dinner from 4 to 11.30pm.

Il Rustico $$ *Rydges Plaza Hotel, Abu Firas Street, Al Bidda, tel: 438 5444.* Italian cuisine in a romantic, rustic-style setting off the Rydges Plaza's atrium lobby. Open for lunch and dinner daily 11am–3pm and 6pm–midnight.

Maxim $$–$$ *Ramada Hotel, Salwa Road, Ramada Junction, tel: 441 7417.* Classic French fine-dining restaurant in a hotel setting near Ramada Junction. Open for dinner daily 7–10.30pm.

Sakura $$$ *Ramada Hotel, Salwa Road, Ramada Junction, tel: 441 7417.* The Ramada Hotel's popular teppanyaki and sushi bar, one of the few options for authentic Japanese cuisine in Doha. Open for dinner daily 7–10.30pm.

Thai Noodles $ *opposite Souq Al Asiery, New Markets/Grand Hamad area, tel: 443 4220.* An excellent-value, no-frills Thai restaurant that offers a selection of international dishes as well as the usual Thai specialities, including red and green curries. A popular *souqs*-area lunch spot, but open throughout the day, every day, from 8am to 11pm.

Turkey Central $ *Al Merqab Street, tel: 443 2927.* An unpretentious, kitchen-style street restaurant serving Lebanese *mezze*, sandwiches, pies, grills and juices. Some of its Eastern hot dishes have a Turkish twist. Excellent value for money enjoyed by a cosmopolitan clientele. Open daily 7am–1am.

WEST BAY

Al Sayyad $$–$$$ *The Diplomatic Club, West Bay Lagoon, tel: 484 7444.* An elegant fine-dining restaurant in exclusive club surroundings on the waterfront in West Bay Lagoon, just to the north of the city. Open for lunch and dinner daily 12.30–4pm and 7pm–midnight.

Al Shaheen $$–$$$$ *Sheraton Doha Hotel and Resort, tel: 485 4816.* Long considered Doha's premier fine-dining restaurant, Al Shaheen now faces stiff competition from other five-star hotel venues, but it still offers the best panoramic view of Doha Bay and the Corniche from its top-floor lookout. Belly-dancing shows twice nightly, and a live band. Open daily 7pm–midnight.

Amigo's $$ *Khalifa Tennis & Squash Complex, tel: 483 7350.* Informal Tex-Mex restaurant and bar. A quiet watering hole in the afternoon, but party central from around 11pm. Live music from a British band. Open daily noon–3am.

Bukhara $–$$ *Khalifa Tennis & Squash Complex, tel: 483 3345.* An atmospheric north Indian restaurant across the road from Amigo's and looking out over the pathways of the tennis centre. Open for lunch and dinner Sun–Wed 11.30am–2.30pm and 6–11.30pm, Thur–Fri 11.30am–3pm and 6pm–midnight, Sat 11.30am–3pm and 6–11.30pm.

Il Teatro $$$ *Four Seasons Hotel, West Bay Complex, tel: 494 8888.* An elegant, ground-level Italian fine-dining restaurant in the plush surroundings of the Four Seasons. Open for lunch and dinner daily noon–2.30pm and 6.30–11.30pm.

La Mer $$$–$$$ *Ritz-Carlton Hotel, West Bay Lagoon, tel: 484 8503.* An elegant, modern French fine-dining restaurant on the 23rd floor of the five-star luxury hotel, offering impressive views of the Arabian Gulf. Open for dinner on weekdays Sun–Tues 6.30–11pm, Wed–Thur 6.30–11.30pm. Gourmet lunch Fri noon–2.30pm, closed Sat.

The Lagoon $$–$$$ *Ritz-Carlton Hotel, West Bay Lagoon, tel: 484 8000.* A light, airy, conservatory-style restaurant with towering palm trees and views of the waters of the Arabian Gulf. Themed buffet nights include Lebanese, Asian with sushi and sashimi, seafood and barbecue, but international flavours of the world predominates. Open for lunch and dinner daily noon–

3.30pm, 6.30–11.30pm. Breakfast also available. A popular venue for Friday brunches.

Le Grill $$–$$ *The Diplomatic Club, West Bay Lagoon, tel: 484 7444.* A steakhouse specialising in grilled marbled steaks and seafood in the elegant surroundings of the Diplomatic Club, located on the coast in the West Bay Lagoon district. Open for lunch and dinner daily 12.30–4.30pm and 7.30pm–midnight.

Lewan $$–$$ *Dana Club, West Bay, tel: 483 4700.* The venerable Dana Club's fine-dining restaurant. Lebanese hot and cold *mezze* and Middle Eastern, oriental and European main courses feature on a varied menu. As it's a club, alcohol is available. Open for lunch and dinner daily noon–3pm and 7pm–midnight.

Paloma $$ *InterContinental Doha, off Aladdin Roundabout, West Bay, tel: 484 4919.* A lively, informal Tex-Mex with rustic-style décor and an outdoor terrace in a five-star resort hotel north of the city. Open for dinner daily 6pm–midnight. Live band. Dancing from midnight to 2am.

Porcini $–$$$ *Ritz-Carlton Hotel, West Bay Lagoon, tel: 484 8000.* Italian fine dining in an elegant but cosy setting. Open for dinner Sat–Tues 6.30–11pm, Wed–Thur 6.30–11.30pm, closed Fri.

Sultan Ibrahim $$$ *InterContinental Doha, off Aladdin Roundabout, West Bay, tel: 484 4444.* Upmarket seafood restaurant set apart from the main hotel in its own building near the beach. Oriental-style seafood and traditional Lebanese fish dishes. Seating on the sea-facing terrace during the cooler months. Open for lunch and dinner Sun–Fri 1–3.30pm and 7pm–midnight, closed Sat.

Za Moda $$ *InterContinental Doha, off Aladdin Roundabout, West Bay, tel: 484 4444.* Contemporary Italian cuisine in an atmosphere that's marketed as 'trendy, informal and fun' – and actually is. Open for lunch and dinner on weekdays Sat–Thur 12.30–3.30pm and 7pm–midnight, Fri dinner only, 7pm–midnight.

INDEX